THE 21ST CENTURY CAREER SEARCH SYSTEM

THE 21ST CENTURY CAREER SEARCH SYSTEM

BRUCE G. GILLIES, PSY.D., M.A., M.S.

© 2016 Bruce G. Gillies. All Rights Reserved.

ISBN 10: 1-942389-07-8

ISBN 13: 978-1-942389-07-1

Published by Prominent Books, LLC

Prominent Books and the Prominent Books logo are property of Prominent Books, LLC.

"Do what you can, with what you have, when you are ready, where you are."

Adapted from Theodore Roosevelt

Table of Contents

Preface 1

Chapter 1
Introduction to Career Patterns in the 21st Century 13

Chapter 2
Why a Career Search SYSTEM? 31

Chapter 3
**Identifying Your Career –
Which Elevator do I Take?** 45

Chapter 4
Navigating YOUR Career Search 73

Chapter 5
Tools of the Career Search 95

Chapter 6
**The Résumé –
Your Career Search Centerpiece** 107

Chapter 7
Communications, Careers, and Control 119

Chapter 8
The Recruiter – Friend or Foe?......................125

Chapter 9
**Use the Web in Your Career Search –
Technology for all of Us**................................133

Chapter 10
**Networking –
Your Best Friend is Your Best Bet**.................141

Chapter 11
The Interview..153

Chapter 12
Negotiating Compensation..........................175

Chapter 13
**Your First 90 days –
Do I Still Have to Work Here?**.......................191

Cover Letter Examples 207

About the Author 221

Other Career Search Tools....................223

References 233

Preface

Today, more than ever, people are looking for careers that not only put bread on their table but also provide them with job satisfaction, a chance for growth, and a future on which they can rely. We live in changing times. Needless to say, technology is the forefront in everything we do. And it's not just the hardware such as phones, computers, satellites, and thermal imaging in cars. Technology is also present in the day-to-day processes we face as well. Customer service representatives are using new processes to ensure we will be a retained customer. Teachers have a better understanding of how to teach and evaluate student learning at all levels through new processes of teaching and learning. And so the process of career search is also impacted by technology as well. We have to change the way we look for careers as much as the new technology forces new careers upon us.

This book is about leveraging technology in process and hardware to enhance your ability to find fulfilling work and work in a career that brings excitement, development, and provides a ladder to success. Life is simply too short to go through it stuck in a horrible job.

Some who purchase this book may be able to dive right into the various tools to investigate their place in the system as they learn how to use them. Others might need to start at the beginning. As an example, if you find that you are getting plenty of interviews but no job offers, you may want to begin with a review of the interviewing and compensation chapters since you've already identified the right career and have an effective résumé and set of cover letters.

This book is for people looking for new careers, people looking for initial entry into careers, and people who need to find a job. Parents of high school students can use this book, transitioning mid-level managers, individuals looking for additional income on top of their primary jobs, or veterans leaving the military. It is designed as a step-by-step process that you can use in a replicable manner for, not only finding your first career, second career, or even third career, but one that can be used time and time again regardless of the economic environment, your individual situation, or career-searching environment. This is not a book of sample résumés or cover letters, although there are several included. Used correctly, this book and system will provide you with a series of tools used to align who YOU are with your vocation and career.

The initial concept of a career requires us to actually define "career". For the purposes of this book, a career can have several definitions. You can, and probably will, have several careers in your lifetime. In the 21st century, it will be the unique individual who can rely on just one career to take them through their entire life. Some will have concurrent careers, such as a surgeon (primary career) who is also a member of the local Rotary Club (volunteer career) and is also on the editorial board of a professional journal (contributory career). Or the school teacher (primary career) who is also an umpire (secondary career) for the local Little League.

You may find that you enjoy working in several different areas. This is absolutely perfect. You will have more energy, more enjoyment, and find relationships much more satisfying when you find a career that you are eager to engage in.

Sadly, many people rely on others to provide them with this engagement in their careers. They wait for their boss to tell them to do something and hope it's interesting. They find their organization does not have the promotion ladder they hoped for or is simply not in alignment with their own values. It is up to each of us, as individuals, to find out what engages us, what starts our motor, what fulfills our need for career satisfaction.

Some may have a primary and temporary career

such as the military, in which one may enlist for 4 years, using this time to explore new career paths. Eventually, a military member may consider the military his or her actual primary career and remain for 20 to 30 or more years, seeking a follow-on career afterwards.

When we look at our strengths and weaknesses and our desired career focus, we sometimes become disappointed in that the career we thought we wanted does not fit with our aptitude, attitude, and skills. We sometimes have to shift our careers due to the life environment we find ourselves in. To find true happiness in a career, regardless of the reason, we must strive to align ourselves with it. We must find our strengths and leverage them to achieve the pinnacle of our career focus.

I've found that the acronym FIRE can provide such a lever for your career search.

FIRE Stands For:

Focus

Intensity

Relationships

Execution

You will find that I reference energy often in this book. Just like with the physical life we live, FIRE gives us this energy. In January of 2000, Martin Seligman proposed a new kind of psychology called "positive psychology." It focused on finding positive individual traits, positive life experiences, and positive attributes that we all have learned from the environment we live in. Using this theory of psychology is a powerful way to improve your career even further. FIRE is one of the surrounding frameworks in which this can operate.

You will need to **Focus** your efforts, control your level of **Intensity**, establish strong **Relationships**, and finally **Execute** the career search system by putting it into motion.

Intended Audience for the Book

This book is not only for individuals seeking work; it is intended to help those individuals who are seeking more than a job. **Veterans** being discharged or retiring from the military will find this book invaluable. Parents of **Graduating high school or college students** trying to understand the steps and process of finding careers will be able to use this book to improve their career and job search skills. **Executives** transitioning between organizations will find key pieces to the search for the next challenging position. Individuals interested in exploring alternate careers to their current career will also benefit from the techniques, processes, and tools in this book.

Organization of the Book

Part one, chapters 1 through 3, will focus on the idea of careers, explaining the new career paradigm in the 21st century. Chapter 1 provides a quick history of careers to provide a platform for the remainder of the book. It will discuss the new career paradigm as experienced by both individuals and organizations. Chapter 2 will focus on the Career Search System, discussing the value of having alignment of the various tools and techniques as a system rather than individual tools to be applied at various times. Chapter 3 discusses the idea of self-control over the career selection process. It reviews various tests and tools that can be used to help identify the best career for individuals. Providing strengths and weaknesses of various assessments, both pen and paper as well as online instruments, it will show the reader the value and limitations of standardized career direction tests.

Part two, chapters 5 through 12, focuses on the various components of a solid career search system. With an overview of résumés and curriculum vitae, tools used to communicate your career aspirations to others, and the technological as well as ad hoc use of these tools. It further discusses the value of recruiters, leveraging the Internet in your career search, the value of networking, and mastering the interview process. This chapter wraps up with an overview of negotiating compensation. Chapter 6 focuses on understanding the use of a résumé and crafting a résumé that will get interviews. Chapter 7 provides details on the various communication tools in the career search process. The controversial topic of recruiters and their value are described in chapter 8, providing the career searcher with key phrases and techniques for maximizing the experience of recruiters. The use of the Internet in the career search is covered in chapter 9, discussing various job search sites, using the Internet in finding out information about careers, and locating organizations that may hold open positions. The value of networking in a career search cannot be overstated. The crafting, developing, and use of a solid network in the career search process is discussed in chapter 10.

Chapter 11 focuses on the key skills involved in effective interviewing and using the technique of "soft control" over the interview process. The issue of compensation is a key element in finding a successful career and simply cannot be over looked. Chapter 12 is dedicated to the notion of compensation and the key techniques to be used to maximize your unique abilities and skills to get the best compensation.

Part Three consists of one chapter, chapter 13, but perhaps the most crucial chapter. It discusses how to determine your person-organization and person-job fit. All of the previous work will likely lead to a position, however, it is the first 90 days in your new career that will set the stage for a pleasurable, engaging, and fulfilling career, or, if it doesn't work, for the position you have just accepted to be "just another job."

The book concludes with a section containing sample résumés, cover letters, typical interview questions, and resources for the career searcher. These resources can be crafted and customized to fit your personalized career search system. They should each be aligned with YOUR career search and not simply copied.

No book is written without the assistance, inspiration, and motivation of others. You will find that I reference several key authors and career scientists throughout this book. Words alone are clearly not enough to inspire and move you to find the perfect career. Consequently, I will provide examples of previous clients and quotes by many of my previous clients, hiring managers, and fellow career counselors to illustrate and explain some of the various concepts. There are various illustrations to bring out key points and models.

What this book is NOT—you won't find a definitive answer in this book to the question: "What should I do for a career?" You won't find the answer to every possible interview question. You won't find that ONE PERFECT RÉSUMÉ.

You WILL find guidance on tools for your career search. You WILL find help in identifying your personal strengths and values. You WILL find examples of excellent résumés, most commonly asked interview questions, and cover letters that get results.

Individuals and organizations reap the benefits of motivated, engaged, and well-designed career searchers. The result is an exciting opportunity for individuals and a highly productive employee for organizations. The career searcher, after employing the concepts, tools, and techniques in this book, will be able to reflect upon their career search experience and use it to evaluate and prepare for a subsequent position within the organization or find a new FIRE to move on to a more fulfilling, engaging, and dynamic career and organization. The developing relationship within the work environment of the 21st century between organizations and their employees defines careers for the future. Organizations will need highly motivated and engaged employees for the challenges of the economy of the 21st century. This book will help provide the 21st century organization with the right employee at the right time.

January 2015
Dr. Bruce G. Gillies

Camarillo, California

Chapter 1

Introduction to Career Patterns in the 21st Century

> I keep six honest serving men
> (They taught me all I knew):
> Their names are What and Why and When
> And How and Where and Who.
> —Rudyard Kipling. *The Just So Stories (1902)*

The 21st Century Workplace

What IS a career? Some define a career as a vocation. Another word might be a "calling" to do a specific job for a lifetime. Some career counselors will tell their clients, "When you find the right career, you'll know it." But how does one go about finding out about the thousands of career fields and whether one has the desire to learn about a specific career, the aptitude to become an expert in a career field, and find out if the compensation in terms of salary, satisfaction, and fulfillment are appropriate.

Finding a fulfilling career is hard work. In fact, it has been likened to a job in and of itself. Finding a new job or career IS a time consuming, emotion laden and financial consideration. Understanding the environment in which the "job of finding a job" is the focus requires us to know a bit about the background of the environment to try to predict where it will be in the near future. So, this chapter will discuss what is meant by the paradigm of a career and how that paradigm has changed over just the past 20 years. But to get to just 20 years ago, let's explore what happened to careers even before that.

Successful career searches in the 21st Century have found that they need to become friends with each of Kipling's "six honest serving men" noted above, asking of them information that leads to the answers they each hold. To this end, it is important to know what the past has held in career systems to better attempt to predict what the future also holds for our careers.

Prior to the industrial revolution, the concept of a career was very different from what it is today. Often, individuals didn't have much choice in the selection of a career. If you were born on a farm in the 1800's, it was likely that you were going to be a farmer for your career. Similarly, blacksmiths, accountants, and even senior management were preordained as the son eventually took over the business from the father, sometimes for several generations. The number of careers was limited due to the confines of travel, communication, and overall rudimentary technology.

In the early 20th century, as technology was increasing in an exponential fashion, careers needed to keep up with the demand. Henry Ford and his assembly line created a need for individuals to learn skills rapidly and retain them to keep up with the demand for the product. Military careers also shifted with "career enlisted" individuals becoming as educated as some officers. Following both of the World Wars, an overabundance of workers led many individuals to innovate new career patterns to meet the needs of a consumer base that demanded new and better products. The proliferation of assembly line productivity throughout the globe and the need for Germany and Japan to re-engage as productive nations required new ways of thinking in terms of management and leadership processes.

Even early in the 21st century, we can see that organizations are much different from the ones that closed out the 20th century. At the end of the last century, computers, although prolific, were not as crucial to business as they are today. The workforce of today has also changed from what we saw in the latter part of the 20th century. From working with many organizations in my consulting business, we have seen more diversity in terms of ".minorities," more women in the workplace and in leadership positions, flexibility in the workplace, and broader scope of responsibility for leaders and managers. In the latter part of the century, during the ".com" boom, it was not uncommon for high-tech workers to find a new job every 90 days.

The employment landscape today has changed even from five years ago. Organizations and individuals are both enjoying more of a "free agent" atmosphere. That is to say job seekers and hiring managers view the fit between the individual and the organization as the focal area. In today's work environment, people might move between organizations frequently. They may sometimes be working for several employers simultaneously. In some cases, individuals who have been downsized move on to other organizations then return to the original one as the needs dictate. What does this mean for the career searcher? This is a distinct change from the career environments of 30 years ago in which employees were expected to stay with one organization.

While, the two-way loyalty between employers and employees is still in existence and valued, it is not nearly as strong as it once was. Human resource laws have caused organizations to be much more cautious in their hiring practices while not hesitating to protect the organization at the expense of an individual employee. This employment landscape offers distinct advantages for the courageous and savvy career searcher.

The pattern for finding and developing successful careers has also changed. In their book *The 5 Patterns of Extraordinary Careers: The Guide for Achieving Success and Satisfaction,* authors James M. Citrin and Richard A. Smith (2005) note that it is no longer enough to simply perform your job to the best of your ability. Developing an internal and personalized career pattern in organizations is also important in career progression. They note that image management and an appreciation for the pursuit of self-actualization are also key contributors to becoming a successful career ladder climber.

Careers today have become a mix of various skills. Careers of the 21st century have changed and become much freer from boundaries. We see employees move from firm to firm as opportunities arise. Organizations downsize then rehire many of their previous employees as consultants. No longer is it sufficient to perform your primary job, such as an accountant, at a very high level for career development and progression. The successful career searcher realizes that in addition to being an expert in their field, regardless of whether they are a newly entered professional or a seasoned, transitioning expert, they must also have additional transferable skills that will contribute to the organization.

Let's take a look at one example of a client of mine from 2005. Doug was 22 when he came to me with a desire to work at a motorcycle shop as a parts specialist. He had been riding motorcycles, working on them, and been to many motorcycling events throughout his life. He decided that he had limited opportunities working for others in the world of motorsports and was looking to expand his options. We sat down and discussed what he liked and did not like about working in the parts department at a motorcycle shop. We were quickly able to focus on the aspects of the job he found most appealing. We were also able to identify his ultimate goal of owning his own motorcycle shop.

Our efforts resulted in a list of primary and secondary skills and knowledge that Doug needed to become an outstanding parts person. He began asking questions of the parts managers around town at the various motorcycle shops; what their experiences were; where they had previously worked; and what they might have done differently were they to start again. Doug quickly discovered that a keen knowledge of parts and which bikes they fit on was actually only approximately 30% of the required knowledge for the position. Being comfortable using computers, inter-personal relationships with other employees, an understanding of how management saw the parts department fitting into the strategy of the company, inventory control, and even a bit of marketing awareness were also needed. This awareness gave Doug a deeper appreciation for the entire scope of the parts management picture. The result of his attempts showed him that his desire to become part of the transportation industry and knowledge of the interrelationship between the parts department was really what he enjoyed.

Within several weeks, Doug shifted his career search to also include car dealerships, trucking maintenance shops, and even several of the airlines in the area. The following month, Doug was hired at a large Chevrolet dealership two cities away as a parts and inventory control specialist. Within two years, Doug was hired on as a parts manager at a multi-line motorcycle dealership 15 miles away from his house. Not only had Doug found his desired career position, but he was now in a position to further his career in the motorcycle industry.

In Doug's case, even though he has not opened his own motorcycle shop yet, he has engaged himself in learning more about the industry and positioning himself to achieve his goal of shop ownership. Without that internal exploration of what motivated him in life, he would not have had the insight to find the career path he ultimately wanted to pursue.

So, what did Doug do correctly? He was open to new opportunities in related fields rather than having his focus too narrow. He realized that his career "dream job" was not going to fall into his lap and that it would take work to achieve. He was able to control the intensity of his drive to achieve his goal so that it was moderated. He developed key relationships within not only the motorcycle industry but also throughout the communities in which he lived.

Unfortunately, not all career searches are so readily successful. Sometimes the needs of family, finances, and fortune can also determine how quickly career searchers need to find employment. It is certainly possible to turn a "job" into a "career." This will take tolerance, flexibility in assignments, and a willingness to take risks.

There are many individuals who started their work at McDonald's and turned it into a full career in hospitality and food service. McDonald's was one of the early organizations to recognize that career development within the organization leveraged the knowledge and experience that their employees had developed. McDonald's "Hamburger University" has a wonderful record of graduating managers and leaders.

BHAG Careers: The Sky's The Limit

Often I find that career searchers have their own, unspoken BHAG (Big Hairy Audacious Goal) careers. We will define a BHAG career as the career you would have if money, time, and energy were not an issue. I often pose a question to many of my younger clients: "What would you spend your time doing if I paid you $100,000 a year to do it?" You may have a BHAG of becoming the CEO of a Fortune 500 company, or the BHAG of working for yourself. Regardless of your BHAG career, conducting research in that field is of prime importance. What are the key skills, education, knowledge, and aptitudes required for your BHAG career? Will its career structure be different by the time you are ready to move on it? How do you position yourself to be prepared for the opportunities in that career field when they appear? The focus of careers is to achieve your career goals. How do you identify your BHAG career and define your own career goals? Nothing says you have to define both of these today. You may end up redefining your career goals and BHAG career as you move forward.

When I was 25 years old, I certainly had no idea I would obtain a Doctorate in Psychology. It did not occur to me until I was 37. Indeed, many of my colleagues do not pursue higher professional aspirations until well into their 30s and 40s.

The following chapters will make use of the six honest men that Rudyard Kipling referred to at the beginning of this chapter. Each of them will contribute to a better understanding of the career search system and how to leverage its strength to achieve career fulfillment.

When comparing the career environment of today to that of the past 50 years, some similarities as well as some glaring differences can be seen. Each stage has different requirements for satisfaction and unique challenges. First, I will provide a well-used set of career stages in Table 1-1. Then, I will provide the new career stages, and then we can take a look at a comparison between the two models. Understanding where you are in your career stage is important in determining the direction of your career.

Table 1-1

20th Century Career Stages

Stage	Growth and Exploration	Establishment	Advancement	Maintenance	Withdrawal
Approximate ages	17-20	21-26	26-40	40-60	60 and older
Characteristics	Testing different jobs. Taking tests to determine career values.	Stressed about competence in their career. Deciding about commitment to career path.	Individuals are independent contributors to organizations. Perform autonomously. Determine long-range career options.	Holding on to career success. Reappraising their career success. Looking for alternate careers to wind up their working life.	Letting go of organizational attachments. Seeking to turn over their knowledge to someone. Evaluating their contribution to society.

In the 20th century model, it followed a fairly linear progression. This was a fairly new paradigm in career progression. The stage of maintenance and withdrawal, as formal stages, were not contemplated during the industrial revolution. People simply worked until they physically could not any longer.

Table 1-2

21st Century Career Stages

Stage	Growth and Exploration	Establishment	Evaluation	Determination	Prospecting
Approximate ages	17-20	21-25	26-35	40-50	55 and older
Characteristics	Testing values, researching different jobs. Cognitively testing occupations.	Obtain first few jobs. Establish self. Tests waters for life satisfaction potential in jobs. Testing boundaries in work.	Evaluating their fit in the world of work. Developing their values. Testing the fit of their values with those of the organization. Determining long-range career options.	Determining how long they want to work. Looking for opportunities. Looking for contribution opportunities and actualizing opportunities. Evaluating what society has become as a result of their efforts.	Checking to see if their mental model of life fits with the free agency original. Looking for consulting opportunities.

As you look at the previous two tables comparing the traditional careers with the careers in the 21st century, several similarities are strikingly apparent. The need for actualization, albeit by different names, is near the end of our life's work. The evaluation stage of the 21st century model is new. This stage in our careers indicates that we are evaluating if we can achieve what we hoped we could and determining whether we need to seek an alternate career (either concurrently or a break from the old one). One point I do want to make here is that the stages may compress or lengthen. Each person's stages in their career may accelerate or slow down depending on their desires, family situation/stage of life, and needs of the career field.

While these stages are relatively consistent across individuals, we must also consider what happens when an individual who might have been in the advancement or maintenance stage suddenly finds himself or herself in the job market as a result of downsizing or other life event. The stages are still there, we just need to adjust and align what we do since age may not directly correspond to the various stages. Someone who was a mid-level manager at 35 years old might suddenly find they have to find another job. They have established themselves as an expert in the field in their organization but now must re-establish their reputation and perhaps take a few steps back and/or a lower level position before being able to gain the momentum necessary to once again move forward.

While it is difficult for individuals who transition from an organization at an advanced career stage, it is equally difficult for organizations to replace corporate or "tribal" knowledge that leaves with those employees. Organizations are becoming increasingly more aware of the impact this loss of knowledge may have and have begun taking steps to ensure that the transfer of this corporate knowledge to others within the organization occurs well before an employee retires. Even employees who are retiring from organizations leave an enormous gap in them. The astute career searcher in an organization will leverage this knowledge and be prepared to step into the position that a retiring manager, leader, or executive might have left.

Our careers are a reflection of us. When asked about who we are, we will typically respond with what we do: "I'm a teacher," or "I fix airplanes." It says very much about us. We must not take this personal identification of who we are lightly. Using all of the resources at our disposal, we must find the right career. The "right" career means the one that provides you with what you want in life. Life is simply too short to go through it with a horrible career. We have the choice. We have the means. It's time to find the RIGHT career for YOU. The 21st century will not wait for you. You have to grab it, shake it, and make it deliver what YOU deserve.

As an old sailor once told me:

"YOU DESERVE WHAT YOU TOLERATE."

Chapter 1 Summary

- The career landscape today has changed from just 20 and even 10 years ago.

- Free agency is seen as a benefit to both occupations and individuals today.

- Opportunities arise. Be ready for them.

- Develop your BHAG career outline.

- Find the answers that the "Six Honest Men" seek.

- Identify your stage in your current career, and align your efforts to maximize that stage's return.

- The stages in the 21st century have shifted.

Chapter 1 Action Plan

List five industries in which you can visualize yourself working for 10 years.

List five companies in your immediate area which employ individuals in your chosen occupation.

Identify your BHAG career including:

- Salary
- Location
- Responsibilities
- Work environment.

Identify your current career stage, and evaluate your level of satisfaction with it.

Chapter 2
Why a Career Search SYSTEM?

"While you can't control the wind, you can adjust your sails."

For many job and career searchers, the challenge of finding a job boils down to one document, their résumé. While a powerful résumé is certainly one of the centerpieces of the career search, it must be crafted so as to leverage the skills of the career searcher, align with the needs of the individual and position they are hoping to get, and finally delivered in front of the right hiring manager at the right time. It cannot do so alone. It is simply one of the components of a career search system.

So why do we call it a system? A system is made up of components that contribute either linearly or in parallel to an end result, often as an intentional synthesis of all the components working together.

One way of looking at the contributions of the components to the system is synergy. Synergy is simply the fact that the end result of many components working together is much more than what the components themselves can do in isolation. We can think of synergy as "synthetic energy," or a factor of the product of the capabilities and limitations of the various "things" that go into the system.

Consider the baggage system in an airport. Each piece of luggage has the goal of meeting up with the correct owner at the end of the trip. The baggage system is comprised of:

1. Acceptance of the luggage from the owner by the airline.
2. Tagging of the baggage.
3. Transportation of the baggage from the terminal to the aircraft.
4. Loading of the baggage onto the CORRECT airplane.
5. Arrival of the airplane safely at the correct airport.
6. Removal of the luggage from the airplane.
7. Transportation of the luggage from the airplane to the terminal.

8. Routing of the luggage to the correct baggage claim carousel.

9. Claiming of the luggage by the rightful owner.

Fortunately, for all of us, airlines have become very adept at making sure this system works correctly. According to the U.S. Department of Transportation's October 2010 Air Travel Consumer Report (which tracked baggage complaints for domestic airlines between August 2009 and August 2010), the overall number of travelers reporting mishandled luggage dropped significantly compared to 2009. An estimated 51 million air travelers flew during the reporting period, and close to 208,000 filed lost, damaged, or delayed luggage baggage complaints with the carriers. While still a large number, it is way down from 2009's total of almost 270,000. Relationally, baggage complaints only represent less than 1%, or 1 baggage complaint for every 250 airline travelers. So, in the bigger picture of this example, it works very well.

However, if just one of those components in the baggage retrieval system fails, your chances of becoming reacquainted with your dirty laundry from the recently completed trip to Hawaii decrease dramatically. Imagine if your luggage tag was torn off either through negligence or design or if there were no trucks or conveyor belts working to offload your luggage from the plane. Well, you get the picture.

Another example is that of the fuel system in your car or truck. The fuel tank stores the fuel, the filter cleans the fuel, the pump delivers the fuel, the piping carries the fuel, and the carburetors or injectors deliver the right amount of fuel to the engine. What happens if your fuel tank is too small for the car? You find yourself filling up all the time and have limited driving range. Or if it's too big, you are carrying around a lot of fuel you might not need, which is bad in terms of weight. If your carburetors or injectors are dirty, the system is inefficient and gets poor mileage, runs roughly, and is unreliable. If any of the components in a system are not working, or not designed correctly in the first place, then the system fails to meet its potential. And so it is with your career search.

Align your career with your career search

Each of the components of your career search, from research to accepting a position and evaluating the organization, must be aligned. The diagram below provides an example of an aligned career search system.

Figure 2-1

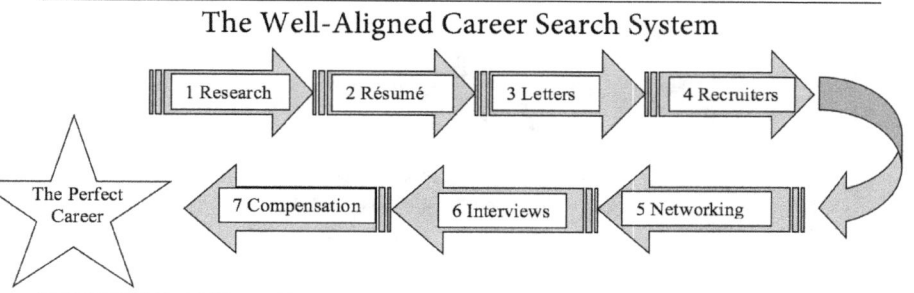

In this diagram, you can readily see that the arrows are aligned, creating a smooth transition from one component to the next. It is very similar to when you are driving your car over a bridge. If the bridge joints are smooth, the car travels smoothly over the bridge. If the bridge joints are misaligned, the ride can be bumpy, inefficient, and uncomfortable. If they are too far out of alignment, the chances for a crash increase and you may never get to your destination. Similarly, in your career search journey, if the components align correctly, the result is a highly rewarding career.

Another useful analogy might be one of a set of gears enmeshed to achieve a final smoothly turning wheel. If the gears are all aligned and working together, the system operates without hiccups. But if just one of the gears is out of alignment, not turning its neighboring gear, or is missing a tooth, the entire set is ineffective.

Figure 2-2

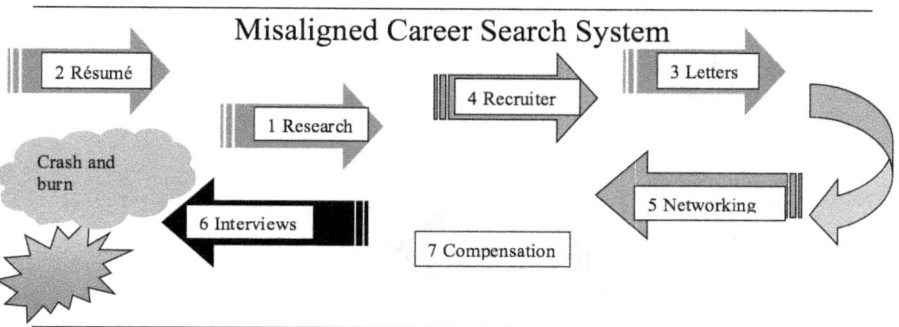

As depicted in figure 2-2, if the components of a career search system are misaligned or they don't have the same FIRE, you are likely to not reach your potential and, in worst cases, end up working in an organization or career where you will find yourself searching for another job. The organization and the individual end up in unsatisfactory situations with disengaged employees, low productivity, and potential litigation shortly down the road.

While your individual system may vary as you continue your career search, it is worthwhile to note that many organizations, outplacement and job search firms are used to this system. Each of these components will need dedicated time from you. Each will need Focus, the right amount of Intensity, the ability to create Relationships, and finally your ability to Execute each of the components. As with any other skill, it is not a quick fix and will likely be a bit rough at the beginning. But the key is to get these components to support one another, work together, and synthesize their strengths to show YOU and your potential in the best possible way.

The significance of each of these components to the larger career search system can be made clearer through an example.

One of my clients was a transitioning senior executive, we'll call Sally. A competitor had recently bought out Sally's company, and senior management had been replaced by the acquiring organization. Consequently, Sally was offered a "Golden Parachute" package, which included significant resources for her outplacement and career search. While Sally's outplacement firm provided an excellent résumé, including a biography (which we will talk about in chapter 6), several formatted letters, and interviewing techniques, it failed to provide her with an overview of the type of organizational values in which she would thrive. Consequently, Sally was hired on at a company in an industry relatively distant from the one she had come from. The organization was highly regulated, and it valued immediate returns on projects rather than long-term improvements. Frustrated, Sally finally came to my office and stated, "If I don't find a better position soon, I'll end up just quitting."

Sally and I sat down and discussed what the challenges were and why she felt the organization was not a good fit for her. We used one of the inventories discussed in this book to help her clarify what her values were in the work place. The company she disliked so very much paid her a competitive salary and had wonderful benefits. However, the individual departments were clearly delineated and left little opportunity for cross-training and strategy discussions between departments. By identifying her values, we were able to find some other organizations that were better suited to Sally's skills as well as her values. This provided her with the FIRE to move forward and investigate other careers. Interestingly enough, Sally found that she enjoyed working in the non-profit sector much more than the Fortune 500. Although she took a 15% pay cut, she found much more enjoyment and fulfilling relationships in the new position.

Sally realized that the type of people who worked in the non-profit industry were there because that was where they wanted to work and not because they HAD to work there. There was a feeling of unity and working toward a common goal. Sally fit in very well and found her passion provided her with, not only a primary job, but also continued offers to present, teach workshops, and write articles, all of which contributed to her financially and professionally.

Clearly the key component in the entire career search system is YOU—the career searcher. Your energy, personality, attitude, and skills are what will determine the ultimate career or careers you find and thrive in. Being able to sustain your energy level for the duration of your career search is going to be one of the most challenging hurdles you will face. Developing and managing your energy level is the key to success. In his landmark book *Good to Great*, Jim Collins (2001) noted the "Hedgehog Principle," in which individuals build momentum through discipline.

Figure 2-3
The Hedgehog Principle

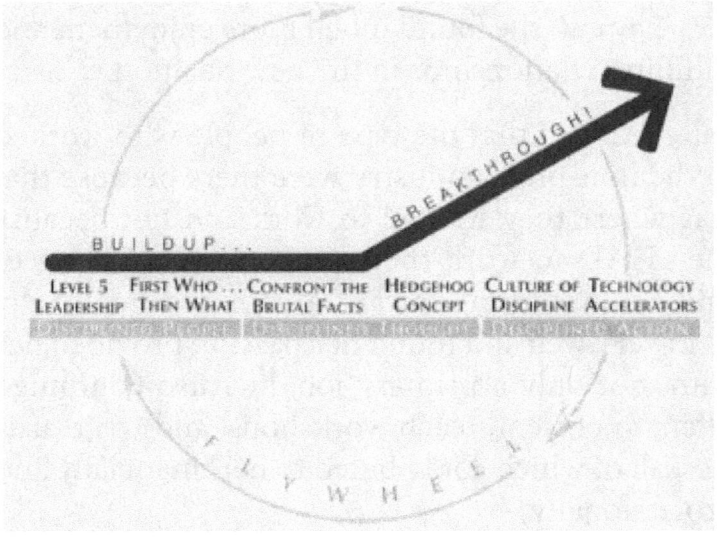

The Hedgehog Principle is based on the premise that there are two types of people in the world: those who are Hedgehogs and realize the value of their assets, and Foxes, those people who jump to rapid conclusions without following through. Foxes pursue many endeavors at the same time and see a complex world that is often overwhelming to the point of paralysis. Hedgehogs simplify the world into various components that need the correct amount of attention before moving on to the next endeavor. Notice that the buildup phase usually takes about half the time to achieve the breakthrough. In your case, you will be building momentum through your research, networking, résumé submissions, interviews, and crafting cover letters.

The Hedgehog Principle notes that it takes disciplined people, using disciplined thought, and executing disciplined action to achieve the breakthrough. Simply throwing résumés out and asking people for work is NOT disciplined, nor is it conducive to a smooth running Career Search System. While the Hedgehog Principle is aimed at organizations, its overarching focus on breakthrough as a result of establishing momentum (such as that developed through the flywheel effect) is one of the key elements in the Career Search System.

You may go for several weeks refining your résumés, crafting cover letters, and attending networking meetings with little to show for your efforts. Then, suddenly, you will achieve a breakthrough and have more offers than you thought possible. I have seen it happen time and time again. It is a perfect example of the Hedgehog Principle at work. Focusing on one component at a time to perfection then leveraging that perfection in the next component is what YOUR career search system is all about.

Chapter 2 Summary

- A system is a series of components working together to bring forth more than just the sum of their parts. They provide SYNERGY.

- Components that are weak or fail within a system impact the reliability and functionality of the entire system.

- Alignment of the components of the system is a crucial piece to ensuring maximum results from your career search efforts.

- Use the correct amount of FOCUS, INTENSITY, RELATIONSHIPS, and EXECUTION (FIRE) to align your components into a full system of career search energy.

- Misalignment can happen if the components are not in the correct order, do not have the right amount of FIRE, or are not organized into a system.

Chapter 2 Action Plan

1. Identify the **FOCUS** of your job search. What are you going to pursue?

2. Plan on how much **INTENSITY** you want to put into your dream job.

3. Identify 4 people you have a **RELATIONSHIP** with who can help you find information on your dream job.

4. Develop a solid plan that will help you **EXECUTE** the first three items in your F.I.R.E. model.

Chapter 3

Identifying and Researching Your Career – Which Elevator do I Take?

"Anyone can find work, but it takes work to find a career."

Selecting a career is not like picking out a new car, a new shirt, or even a new romantic relationship. We cannot just select a career from out of a hat and hope it fits. We also need to maintain a specific amount of control in our lives in order to be able to not only survive the career search but to thrive in it and learn more about ourselves. The best way to do this is to be proactive rather than reactive. I had a teacher who once told me:

"There are three kinds of people in this world.

Those who watch things happen (reactive),

those who make things happen (proactive),

and those who wonder "WHAT THE HECK HAPPENED?" (confusion)."

Being proactive means going out and finding information on specific careers you are considering rather than hoping something will fall into your lap. To find a GREAT career, you will need to know something about yourself. You will need to be proactive in finding out what you like, what you do not like, and what you are willing to tolerate in order to get to what you are passionate about.

One example is a small business owner for a candle shop who really enjoys designing and making wonderfully scented, beautifully crafted candles. The candle maker enjoys it so much, he decided to make this his career. Of course, if you are going to sell candles, you have to account for the money, market the business, hire staff, and a myriad of other details that come along with running a business. The candle-stick maker realizes that in order to enjoy his passion and make a living from it, he needs to have a level of tolerance and become competent at the other things that make a business successful but are not always the most fun.

This effort of finding out about your preferences, potential careers, and gaining information relates to the "research" portion of the Career Search System:

Figure 3-1

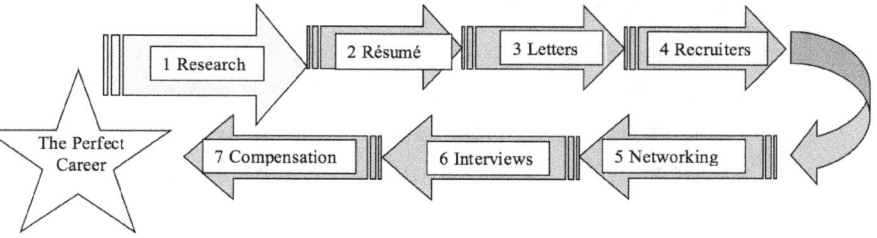

The research stage is quite likely THE most important stage in your career search process. All of the other components in this system rely on your perpetual, accurate, and dedicated research into finding out who you are, what you can do, what you like to do, where you should work, and what strengths you possess.. No other aspect of the system can take the place of thorough, novel, and investigative research into a variety of careers.

Even if you are currently employed, you should still keep your antenna tuned for new careers. After all, in 1974, who would have predicted that one could make money designing websites? In truth, if you told someone in 1974 that you were a website developer, they would have signed you up for a class in pesticide application. "Get rid of the spiders then."

You will also want to investigate and research the ultimate and potential outcomes of your careers of interest. What kind of things can come from your ideal successful career? Perhaps you want fame, fortune, friends? Those can be rewarding. But also fulfillment, stability, and enjoyment are outcomes of a successful career. Once you begin to distill this process down and find out what values you hold most dear and what values you absolutely reject, you will have a much clearer picture of your perfect career.

One of the areas that confuse quite a few of my clients is identifying their passion. Many feel they simply cannot, or more specifically will not, find a career that encompasses their passions. Often, I find that these clients have the idea that work must be distasteful or that you cannot mix pleasure and work. A few have said they do not understand what we mean by "passion" for a vocation.

Figure 3-2, the Career Search Focus Union, shows there are three major things to explore when considering a career: passion, outcomes, and potential. Your "passion" is labeled in the triangle, "where do your passions lie?" The outcomes are in the, "what do you want out of your career" rectangle. And your "potential" is in the, "what can you be the best in the world at" circle.

Let's take a look at the triangle. What does it mean to have a passion about something? Some say it means "to fall in love with it." The goal of finding a wonderful career is to find one that you DO fall in love with. When you do what you love, you will wake up with excitement and enthusiasm to start each workday. You will want to stay beyond the end of the workday. You will take joy in telling others what you do and what you are working on. There is little that can match the joy and fulfillment that comes with being in the RIGHT career.

Figure 3-2 The Career Search Focus Union

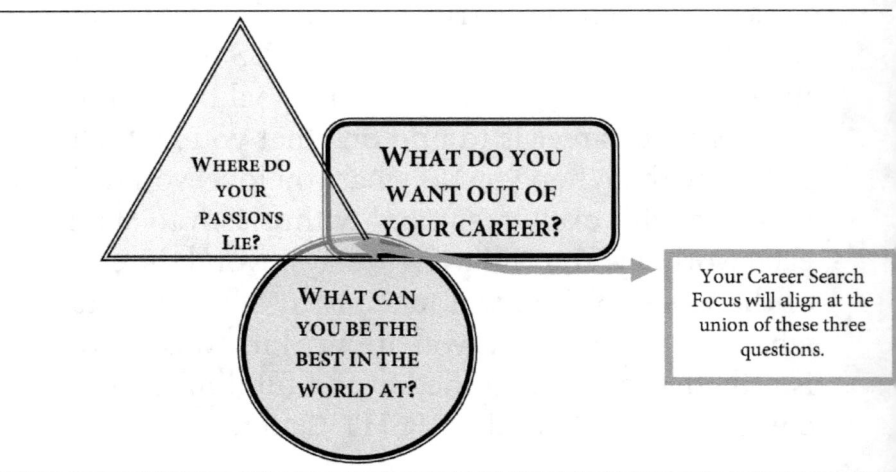

As you can see, there are several questions that must be answered before we can really begin to research specific careers. Many of you might say, "What do you mean, 'What do you want out of a career?' Isn't that what this book is all about?" And to a point, the answer is yes. This book is designed to help you focus your energy on career search and obtaining the "right" career for you. This chapter will discuss many opportunities and tools to help you find the answers to these questions.

Let me bring out one important point. Note that in the paragraph above, I stated "...obtaining the 'right' career for you." I did not say the "best" career for you. The right career can certainly be the best career for you. However, the "right" career is the one that fits you. The best career may be one that requires so much sacrifice on your part that you simply consider it not worthwhile.

In one of my favorite movies, *Miracle*, about the 1980 Olympic Hockey team, Herb Brooks, the new coach, was reviewing the selection of 25 players from a pool of about 60 candidates. His assistant coach, Craig Patrick, reviewed the list and told Herb, "These aren't even the best players you picked."

To which Brooks replied, "I don't want the BEST players; I want the right ones." The right ones who would fit in with his style of play could tolerate his style of practice and would behave in the right manner with their teammates.

Your career search is not much different. The RIGHT career is the one YOU want. The BEST career is a determinant of so many other factors. What may be the BEST career for compensation might be a brutal career for family life due to travel. The BEST career for family life might be one that requires slow promotion opportunities. You can see that BEST can be translated in many different ways, while the RIGHT career is up to you.

Successful career searchers are always on the lookout for new opportunities. The focus of their awareness is to have their radar tuned to opportunities rather than having the opportunities come to them. One example is of a client of mine. She was a marketing manager who recently was downsized due to a geographic shift in her organization's strategy. She was a highly qualified individual, and the only reason she was offered the downsizing package was due to the level at which ALL employees were outplaced. She was at the level in the organization at which the company decided to downsize ALL employees. We'll call her Candace. While Candace was in the midst of her outplacement efforts, she had several individuals ask her what she did. When she told them she was a marketing manager, they offered her consulting opportunities. Rather than turning them down as not being "real employment," Candace leveraged these contacts into consulting work, which in turn resulted in a solid network upon which she could draw for future consulting and employment opportunities.

I asked her, "What do you consider the most important thing that contributed to the opportunities coming your way?"

She smiled and said, "I really think that by keeping a positive attitude, people are more likely to see you as an asset to their efforts." This illustrates a great lesson to be learned.

Finding the Right Elevator

An elevator, like stairs, gets you to the right place in a building. However, if you take an elevator, you have to make sure that it stops at the right floor for you. I have seen some elevators that start at the 14th floor of a 30-floor building, so if you get on and need to get off at floor ten, you are in for some stairs. Similarly, if you get on an elevator that will not take you high enough, you will have to get off the elevator when it stops.

The point is, select a career that will get you to the level that is right for you in terms of achievement, recognition, income, and flexibility. Picking the right floor to get off at is what we are talking about. To determine that, you need to figure out how much time you have, how much effort you are willing to put into it, and if the outcomes are going to be equal to the amount of perceived effort you have to put into it.

One way of looking at this comes from the motivational model called "Expectancy Theory." In 1964, Victor Vroom developed his theory in an attempt to help explain motivation in the workplace. He suggested that people are motivated to strive for a specific goal in relation to the value to the individual, the effort required to achieve the desired outcome, and the expected outcome itself. Expectancy theory states that when confronted with a decision on whether to pursue a given end or not, we will compare what we have to put into it with what we expect to get out of it. Without getting too far into the minutiae of the theory, it basically means that we assign a value to the expected outcomes of our efforts, in this case career search. We then evaluate whether we perceive it is worth it to us to pursue that goal. Will the amount of effort we put into pursuing a career be worth the outcomes of the career in terms of what we value?

Imagine a young high school student who watches the television show *Grey's Anatomy* and wants to pursue a career as a surgeon. The outcomes, as exhibited in the show, are very appealing—great work environment, fun coworkers, drama, helping save people, and the salary that comes with being a surgeon. Heck, you even get to specialize in a specific part of the body. What's not to like about THAT? Well, our young friend begins to explore what it takes to become a surgeon … okay, so we need to take college classes in biology, anatomy, chemistry … lots of people get through college. Oh, and then there are the four additional years of medical school, sometimes more. "Do I get to practice medicine yet?" No, not quite yet. Now you get to do your residency and internship—a five to seven year process.

By this time, most teenagers (yes I do have one, and more on their way into that stage) will say, "WOW, so after high school I have another (counting on fingers) 13 to 15 years before I can even practice medicine on my own? That's just so totally NOT worth it." In this case, the expected outcome values exceed the input values in terms of time and opportunity for other more "valuable" things.

However, let's say your young teenager says, "I would like to get into medicine."

First question a parent should ask is, "Why?" We hope we would get a very altruistic answer like, "To help make people feel better," or, "To support those who need it." Sometimes we might get the "flexible hours" answer, but at a semi-cognitive level, they are also evaluating how much time and effort it will take. The fact is they can become a nurse's assistant or nurse's aide fairly quickly then progress up the nursing professional scale to eventually obtain their Nurse Practitioner certification. This process takes several years less than that of a surgeon. But to be fair, the potential salary outcomes of a nursing career, even at its peak, are not up to what a good surgeon can make.

So, when evaluating the career field you are exploring, find out what it takes to get there. Is the journey, with its various hurdles, snags, and mountains to climb, going to provide you with too much of a challenge? Be honest with yourself. Starting off on a journey in which you do not have the resources is going to be an experience in frustration and futility.

And remember that the career process is indeed a journey. Even the path to becoming a brain surgeon, piloting a 747, or being the CEO of a Fortune 500 company has many valuable and enjoyable lessons along the way. A career search can be seen as not only a system, but as a journey as well.

The Career Shift

One paradigm shift that has happened in the past 30 years in terms of careers is the notion of a "lifelong career." While it is certainly possible that you might pick the right career for yourself early in life and stay with that career your entire life, it is not uncommon to find individuals who picked a career and enjoyed its fruits for a while but now want to try something different. These career "shifters" have found that the key to an enjoyable life is to have a life full of experiences. There is nothing wrong with shifting careers. In fact, some careers cannot be entered into until you have experienced much in the way of other careers. An example is that of a career counselor. My own experience has brought me through several "careers" before finding Career Counselor as my vocation. Experiencing the journeys of my previous careers gives me the opportunity to advise others on specific aspects of careers. Another career that requires extensive experience is that of management consultant. You would need to have experience in working with a variety of organizational problems and experience with several organizations to be a truly effective management consultant.

Earlier, we discussed the concept of a career "elevator." I think it bears discussing that while you can certainly climb the ladder of career success, there is nothing like a solid education that will give you the elevator lift to achieving it. It does not matter much if you are a carpenter, a nurse, or a printer. Getting a solid education is one of the fastest and most effective ways to get to that sweet spot of a career. Once you have your education, formal or informal, no one can take that away from you. Often I have clients who have not even considered the opportunities that an education might bring them. So explore, educate, and expedite your career with your education. The means are there through a myriad of government programs. The motivation, however, MUST be yours.

Careers and Family Values

What is the "real deal" on work/family balance? Do women have to give up their professional career aspirations to raise a family? Many women exited the workforce to raise families and, either due to divorce or empty nest, now find that they need to revisit the employment question and explain their employment gap. Nowadays, more men are choosing to stay home or share more fully in the "day-to-day" raising of a their families, and, as a result, they are in a much different position than their fathers, many of whom were expected to sell their souls to advance in the company and leave raising the family to their wives.

Much has been said and written on balancing family life with a professional career. Both men and women face many daily decisions that make an impact on both: "Do I work Saturday because the boss wanted me to finish a project, or do I attend my son's little league game?" "Do I take that business trip or stay home to attend my daughter's first Christmas play?" and in some cases, even larger decisions such as, "Do I take the job in New Zealand? My son is only 7 years old." The good news is that many organizations today are starting to realize the value of making sure there is a solid family-work balance. However, the challenge still remains for many men and women today of balancing both a professional career outside the home with their own values of what it takes to raise a healthy family.

Women and Professional Careers

The "glass ceiling" refers to an invisible barrier preventing some individuals from advancing to higher levels within an organization due to gender, ethnicity, or sexual orientation. Unfortunately, the "glass ceiling" is still present in many organizations. Although it is beyond the scope of this book to attempt to address the number of issues a "glass ceiling" represents for both organizations and its employees, or how individuals might overcome the advancement limitations imposed by a "glass ceiling" environment, I believe organizations that limit the advancement of qualified individuals are ignoring the variety of opportunities and innovations that a diverse and varied workforce may bring. Detecting this glass ceiling is a difficult task. At what level does it start to take effect? Do I want to go above that level? Many individuals are satisfied working beneath the glass ceiling. Sadly, when those individuals find that the ceiling is there, they often give up ... DON'T!!! Once you find that an organization has a glass ceiling and it is beyond your value system to accept it, or your ability to change it, move on to another organization. If you have the people skills, the technical skills, the drive, the motivation and, most importantly, the desire, other organizations WILL find your value and use your talents. While it can be a bit unnerving when planning that move, a contingency plan for it will pay dividends in the long run.

Re-entering the Work Force

"When you come to a fork in the road, take it." – Yogi Berra (2002)

The educational journey can be started at any time in life. I was the director of an adult education program at a university in California. I had many students who decided to come back and obtain their degrees after 10, 20, 30, or more years in the workplace. The record was a gentleman who came back at 55 years of age and finished his Bachelor's degree at 72. A true testament to "Life-Long Learning." The lesson to be learned in this section is that it is NEVER too late to evaluate your career options and make adjustments to pursue YOUR desires. Our average life span is longer today than at any other time in our history. People "retiring" at 65 still have another full career they can pursue if they would like. Your task is to evaluate where you are in your career progression and life goals and see what it might take to adjust to achieve these goals.

Culture and Companies – Best Companies to Work For

Let's discuss one of the characteristics of a career that is common to virtually every career out there—the organization. It a variable that you typically do not even think about when you consider your career search, yet it is an important one. What was a great career in the beginning of the 20th century, such as perhaps a job at the newly formed Ford Motor Company or perhaps the railroad, would be seen as undesirable labor today. Times change, organizations change, and, of course, people change.

To a large degree, the company you work for will determine the level of career satisfaction you experience. Some companies are known for the way they take care of their employees, others gain a reputation for how tough they are on their workforce. The alignment of your values and your own career aspirations with those of the organization you work for will also determine your level of satisfaction within a career. Organizations with an excellent reputation for taking care of its employees are known for the benefits, career development opportunities, the level of autonomy given to its employees, and the way the organizational leadership views the fit of the employee base with the organizational strategy. When you can, you should view the entire list of the top 100 companies to work for at:

http://fortune.com/best-companies/

Here is the Fortune list of the top 10 companies to work for in the U.S. in 2015:

Table 3-1

Ranking	Company	Location
1	Google	Mountain View, CA
2	The Boston Consulting Group	Boston, MA
3	ACUITY	Sheboygan, WI
4	SAS Institute	Cary, NC
5	Robert W. Baird	Milwaukee, WI
6	Edward Jones	St. Louis, MO
7	Wegmans Food Markets	Rochester, NY
8	Salesforce	San Francisco, CA
9	Genentech	South San Francisco, CA
10	Camden Property Trust	Houston, TX

Each of these companies is not necessarily the most profitable in their industry, although Google seems to be doing quite well, nor are they the biggest organizations in the world. But they do have several key factors going for them that have worked, and they manage to turn a profit.

As you research each of these companies, and the company for which you want to work, remember that the career and employment landscape changes from year to year. You will need to determine if you think your BHAG career would have an organization that fits with your values.

We will discuss values a bit further on into the book as we explore what it takes for people to find a career that is fulfilling and dynamic. Will ALL employees in each of these companies say they have the best job in the best company? Out of the more than 68,000 employees who are working for them, the answer will not be a unanimous cry of unadulterated glee at working there. There are some people who will not fit in with the culture of even the BEST companies. They might simply need more, or less, structure, a bit more direction from their supervisor, or more opportunities for promotion. What YOU may decide is the best company to work for is most likely different from the company I decide is the best fit for me.

Informational Interviews

Let's not forget that the most current sources of information about various careers are individuals who are working in these career fields now. We will be discussing informational interviews in a later chapter as part of the overall interview process, but it bears discussing now as an essential component in the research tool. The key is to be able to spend an hour with an individual who is approximately mid-career in the occupation you believe you might enjoy. When conducting these informational interviews, timing is everything. It is probably not a great idea to stop a pilot on their way to a flight to see if they can tell you what they like and do not like about their job. You may be in for a rude surprise if you attempt to get a police officer to stop in the middle of giving someone a citation to chat about their career progression. However, by and large, people like to talk about what they do.

Many organizations have a website with points of contact. There are also a lot of professional associations that are more than ready to chat with you in hopes of getting you to join their career. One great example, and a wonderful resource for career searching, is the Society for Human Resource Management (SHRM). SHRM is well known throughout the various occupations within human resource management as a certifying organization as well as a resource for organizations.

Regardless of the profession, there are numerous individuals out there who would LOVE to talk with you. But you must take action to set up the interview, and be considerate of their time.

Researching Specific Companies

After you have completed your research on the various careers you would like to explore, you may find that, although you have certain aptitudes, a specific industry might hold more of an attraction than a specific occupation. Furthermore, you may find that a specific company holds your interest and you are willing to see if there are any jobs within the company that you might be qualified to do. One excellent resource for finding information on the work environment of various companies is www.glassdoor.com. It provides an inside look at different occupations and companies, and also has a salary comparison tool. In some instances, employees, as well as former employees, provide feedback on the leadership team, organizational culture and environment, and other factors.

The value of conducting research through the company's own website cannot be overstated. Similar to the non-verbal cues we pick up from others, a great deal of insight can be gained by reviewing what is and what is not said on a company's website. How much effort do they put into the company's "face" of their website? Is it easy to navigate? Can you readily find information? While it is possible that a company may be wonderful to work for but have a crude, less-than-dynamic website, it is more likely that the company's face is actually representative of how they conduct business. A difficult to navigate website is likely indicative of an organization that will be difficult to navigate your career in as well. I have found some organizations that do not even have a phone number posted on their website, which makes you wonder how they get business.

While the above resources and websites are helpful in finding out about occupations when you have decided on what occupation to research, there are many resources available to help you determine which occupation you might be best suited to pursue. These resources come in many forms including books, websites, films, and even people you know.

One of the foremost books on career search, now in its 43rd anniversary edition, is *What Color is Your Parachute?* In this landmark book, Richard Bolles (2013) does an excellent job of providing insight and tools on career search. While "parachute" is focused on the career search process and discusses much in the way of personality and careers, it does not have as much focus as the Career Search System on specific tools. However, I highly recommend it as an addition to your career search tool kit.

Remember that these tools are simply that—tools. They will not provide you with all the answers and must be interpreted correctly, either by you or by an expert in the field. Your ability to learn from these tools and apply what you have learned to the alignment of YOU and your potential career is what is most important. ***Know Thyself.*** There is no one out there who will take better care of YOU than YOU. Once you have taken care of yourself and found your ideal career, you will be in a much better place to take care of your loved ones. While this may seem a bit selfish, you will find it to be very true. If you rely on others to take care of you, you will be disappointed. If you try to take care of others before you take care of yourself, you will not only resent the effort it takes, but you will also let others down.

Starting Your own Business

It is entirely possible that your passion and drive will not be found in another organization or industry. Perhaps you have a unique set of skills that is not apparent in many large or even medium businesses. It is to these people that I want to provide a few thoughts on the value of starting and running your own small business. In 2011, the Small Business Administration (www.sba.gov) reported "Small Businesses," or more appropriately "Small Firms," accounted for 99.7% of all employers in the United States. (It should be pointed out that not all organizations are called "businesses" since some small firms are not-for-profit or "non-profit" organizations.) These "small businesses" are mom-and-pop restaurants and small or home-based businesses in which entrepreneurs sell the inventions or innovations they have created.

While the risks of owning a small business are not for everyone, it can be a lucrative occupation that can be done in your spare time while searching for that permanent and fulfilling career or while working for another employer. The rewards of small business ownership are enormous. The satisfaction of following your dream and being successful are often well worth the extra effort. You are able to bask in the glory of a successful business but are also the one everyone expects to exemplify a less than optimal business experience.

There are many opportunities and advantages to starting your own business, even as a side business. Various tax benefits can be aligned with being your own business owner, even as a part-time business venture. For more information, check with your local Small Business Administration office, Small Business Development Organization, and county offices.

There are loans and grants available for starting up or expanding small businesses. Depending on your business model and objectives, the possibility that a venture capitalist may find your business attractive and offer funding to get it off the ground also exists. There are a number of retired senior businessmen and women looking for opportunities to share their business acumen and knowledge. The Service Corps of Retired Executives (SCORE) is a network supported by the Small Business Administration (SBA), which consists of many business executives who provide free coaching and mentoring to individuals who would like to start their own businesses.

Ultimately, exploring careers arms you with information. This information is as good as gold when trying to find out what career, industry, or jobs you are interested in. Getting stuck in an uncomfortable career is a waste of your energy, your life, and your time.

Chapter 3 Summary

Careers and their research will take a large portion of your efforts when investigating the career you want to pursue.

There are many instruments and tools. Make sure the tool you, or the career professional you have engaged with, use is a valid measure for career search purposes.

Career search instruments can measure:

- Personality
- Values
- Aptitudes
- Skills

No one can tell you invariably the absolute best career for you. You must evaluate the information for yourself.

Consider starting your own business. You have a marketable skill at some level. Explore it.

Chapter 3 Action Plan

- Select 3 jobs that you would ABSOLUTELY NOT WANT. Why? What component of your dream job are they missing?

- Evaluate your desire to work for others. Do you need direction in your work? Are you a self-starter, or do you need a kick-start every now and again?

- List five values that an occupation you are considering MUST have. This may also include, "An organization within an industry of interest."

Chapter 4
Navigating Your Career Search

Occupation and Career Theories

So exactly what IS a career? There are many career theories out there. Some were designed in isolation at a specific time within our history while others seem to have weathered the myriad of changes we have seen in the past 30 years and are still applicable today. Some are based on personality, others on skill and aptitude. Of the personality-based theories, probably the one that has endured and is most prevalent, even today, is John Holland's Occupational Themes theory (RIASEC).

In 1959, John Holland developed a theory regarding the aptitude of individuals for specific types of careers. He designed a hexagonal (six sided) tool that categorizes jobs into specific types that were determined by the type of work they do. The six types are:

- Realistic
- Investigative

- Artistic
- Social
- Enterprising
- Conventional

Figure 4-1

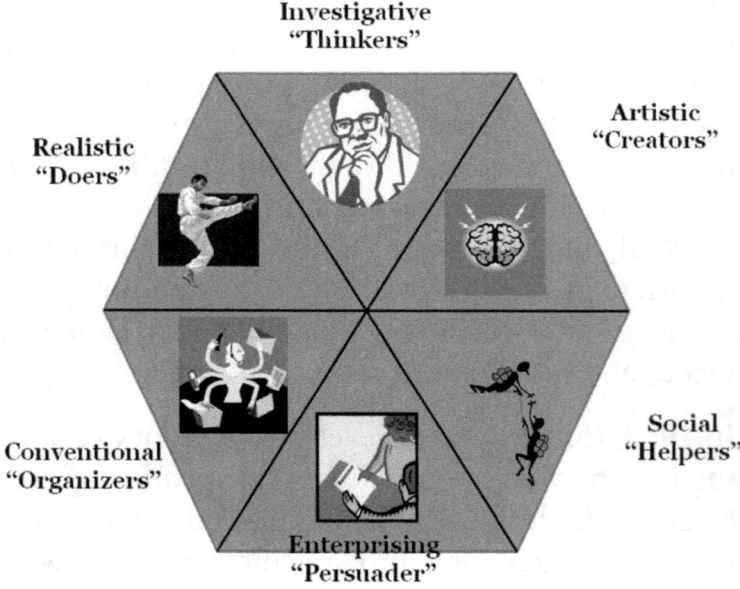

Virtually any job can be placed into one or more of these occupational categories. Some may be a 50-50 split between two, others may have a little bit of each in them. The key to using Holland's job types is to find out what kind of person you are and what values you hold. Your personality and skills must be aligned with the type of career you are searching for to ensure that you find a fulfilling career.

As an example, an individual who is very friendly, outgoing, and likes to meet new people would be very well suited to a career in the "social" (highly developed human relations competencies such as interpersonal and social competencies) category. However, if you put that same person into an occupation in the "realistic" category (working with explicit, structured, systematic manipulation of tools, machines, and objects,) they would likely be miserable.

You might say, "Well what if I like working with both?" Which is certainly possible and true for many people. Indeed there are many occupations in which the various categories cross reference each other and support two or more of the occupational areas. An excellent example of someone who enjoys the realistic aspects as well as the social aspects might be someone who is in the field of sales for equipment, large construction machinery, cars, or aircraft.

Tests and Instruments to Help Determine Which Careers are Best Suited for You

I can hear the wheels in your head turning. "Okay, so how do I find out which RIASEC occupational field I have the most characteristics in?" The instrument that will give you your own RIASEC report is called the RIASEC Personality Test. Many career counselors, career centers, and psychologists have access to this instrument. There are also several online resources you can use to take the RIASEC personality inventory. The "Big Job Portal" is an excellent resource and provides a free RIASEC personality inventory for you to take:

http://www.bigjobportal.com/riasec/

While the results may provide a categorized list, I highly recommend you take those results to an experienced career counselor to help you interpret them to determine how they might fit with your own perceptions of what a successful career might be.

The use of assessment instruments by career seekers and career professionals is broad and varied. At one point, I found more than 150 different career counseling tests and assessment tools that were available to help individuals find their "calling." While it is beyond the scope of this book to investigate each and every one of them, we will take a look at some of those that are the most prevalent and provide the most accuracy.

Personality Measurement Tools

Remember that the RIASEC personality inventory is just that—a personality inventory. I have identified it early in this section because it is career focused and well accepted in the career counseling field. It does have some limitations in that it is a self-report instrument similar to many other personality tools. There are other personality tests that can help you identify your personality type. Below is a short list of those I have found most helpful:

The DiSC – (Dominance, Influence, Steadiness, Conscientiousness)

This is one of my favorite personality type indicators because it does not profile you by saying you have only one of several types of personalities. Rather, it provides you with a report on what type of environment you work best in. As an example, the DiSC provides you with the way you might prefer to receive feedback from a performance appraisal, the type of people you work best with, and the amount of structure you might need. Also, rather than simply stating what "kind" of personality you have, it offers a very nice narrative that provides more insight. This is helpful to the career search as you are exploring careers and learning of the environments in which they are most often found. Granted, some organizations within specific occupations will vary greatly, but the DiSC also provides you with an idea of the organizational culture in which you will also be best suited.

The NEO-PI – (Negativity, Extraversion, Openness – Personality Inventory)

The NEO-PI is a good tool to use to identify the strengths and weaknesses you have relative to the Five Factor Model of Personality. The NEO-PI report will provide an overview of your values on the five different personality factors of Neuroticism, Extraversion, Openness, Agreeableness, and Conscientiousness. A good way to remember these five types of personality characteristics/factors is the acronym OCEAN. A brief explanation of each follows.

Neuroticism (Sometimes Called Negative Affectivity)

This scale provides you with the amount of discomfort and stress you may feel as a result of negative events in your life. Do you let small things get you down? If you break a fingernail, is your day totally shot? Then you would have a high level of negative affectivity. On the other hand, if having a car accident on the way into work is just a bump in the road, or if a divorce is merely a hiccup in your relationship history, then you will have a low level of neuroticism.

Extraversion

To what extent are you comfortable with meeting new people? Do you actively seek out new relationships? Or are you more of the shy type who prefers to be left alone? Clearly this will have a major impact on your career decision. Someone who is very low on the extraversion scale would probably not make a very good automotive sales person. On the other hand, someone who is very high on the extraversion scale would likely not be very happy as an accountant spending large amounts of time with a computer and numbers rather than others.

Openness

Individuals high on the openness scale generally have very active imaginations and seek out new experiences. They seek out others' opinions about these experiences. Someone who is high on the openness scale may be an excellent candidate for exploratory jobs in art, some sciences, and other creative-type occupations. A website designer would likely have a high level of openness as they explore the various ways of creating and designing a website. On the other hand, someone who has a relatively low level of openness might be better suited to traditional jobs that are relatively structured with few surprises and little variety.

Agreeableness

Individuals who have a high level of agreeableness are often very comfortable in social situations in which there may be a large amount of contentious topics. Do not be mistaken; these are not "yes" men/women. If you have a high level of agreeableness, you are probably one who seeks social harmony and are likely able to have a high level of empathy. A position in which understanding and satisfying clients' needs might be very rewarding for you.

Conscientiousness

A high level of conscientiousness can be likened to a "High level of attention to detail." Individuals high in conscientiousness are dutiful in following rules and regulations, very organized, time driven, and thorough. Individuals high in conscientiousness would find themselves very comfortable in a highly regulated industry that has clear expectations, many rules, and is structured. They require an uncanny knack for precision. Typical occupations for those high in conscientiousness include engineers, pilots, and law enforcement.

Keep in mind that for each of the five factors

mentioned above, you will not be listed as just one of them, such as "EXTRAVERT." You will have a specific amount of each factor, with some being very strong while others are comparatively low. As with any instrument, I encourage you to sit with a career counselor who can help you interpret the results of the NEO-PI.

MBTI – Myers Briggs Type Indicator

The MBTI and its underlying theory of psychological types was developed by C.G.Jung (1971). It provides a method of distilling an individual's personality down into 16 types based on 4 distinct categories. These categories are:

- *Extraversion or Introversion (E vs I)*
- *Sensing or Intuition (S vs N)*
- *Thinking or Feeling (T vs F)*
- *Judging or Perceiving (J vs P).*

When you take the MBTI, you will receive one of 16 four-lettered identifiers for your personality or "type" from these four categories of seemingly opposite values. The chart below provides you with the 16 possible types:

Chart 4-2

ISTJ	ISFJ	INFJ	INTJ
ISTP	ISFP	INFP	INTP
ESTP	ESFP	ENFP	ENTP
ESTJ	ESFJ	ENFJ	ENTJ

These sixteen types of personalities, of which you are one, will provide you with a set of values that you are presumed to have. The MBTI has been used by many organizations to determine fit. As a career direction tool, while limited, it can provide you with a quick perspective on your personality type. In addition, it can offer you an idea of who you might like to work with as well as the generalized environment that might suit your personality.

Kiersey-Bates Temperament Sorter

Another similar instrument is the Kiersey-Bates Temperament Sorter. It uses the same basic 16 personality types as the MBTI, with the following changes:

- The MBTI focuses on how people think while the Kiersey focuses on behavior.
- The Kiersey-Bates focuses more on a field theory model in a larger systems approach.

- Kiersey-Bates sorts individuals into four "Temperaments" of:
    - Idealist
    - Rational
    - Guardian
    - Artisan

Values-Based Instruments

While the above instruments measure personality, you must also consider what values you embrace. Values are those things that tell you what is good and what "should" be the correct viewpoint. Generally speaking, they are those "things" that people want to attain or seek to satisfy. Values-based career searching helps you most closely align those careers with your values. The link of having aligned values between you and your career is significantly related to your level of job satisfaction.

In contrast to a personality instrument, a values-based instrument helps you identify what your values are and provides you with a map of careers that most closely matches your own values. As an example, you might value being able to work alone. This value would be in contrast with a team-focused career such as an operating room. You may also value helping others who may be less capable of helping themselves in your organization. This would be a great value in alignment with an organization that also values the same assisting type of behaviors. Ultimately, values are what drives our behavior. Two individuals may have very similar personalities but value different things. One might value driving for extreme power and financial success while another values self-sufficiency and quiet times.

Lets take a look at some values-based instruments and how they might assist in your career search system.

SYMLOG – System for Multi-Level Observation of Groups

While this instrument seems to be labeled as a way of looking at groups, it is also an excellent tool in terms of identifying your own values as they are related to a "norm", or generally accepted set of values and behaviors. It helps you, as an individual, integrate your values with those of groups. It places your values on one of three major dimensions:

- Dominance versus Submissiveness
- Acceptance of Established Authority
- Friendliness

One aphorism from the www.symlog.com website:

"You are measured:

> • not by what you are, but by the perception of what you seem to be

> • not by what you say, but how you are heard

> • not by what you do, but how you appear to do it

> • and, most importantly, not by what you intend, but by your actual effect on others." — (Anonymous)

This speaks quite loudly about the importance of values and their subsequent behaviors in the world of work. Just like the various tools of the Career Search System, the alignment of your values to those of the career and organization you select will determine your level of career satisfaction and potential.

In Figure 4-3, note that the vertical axis provides the importance of accepting or rejecting established authority, the horizontal (left-right) axis provides values on friendly or unfriendly behavior, and the size of the bubble dictates the level of dominance (larger is more dominant).

Every occupation will have values that differ as far

as what it takes to be successful in each of these three dimensions. A career in the military might require a stronger set of values that contribute to "accepting task orientation of established authority," while an artist might be seen as someone who moves away from that same dimension because they require more creativity to be successful.

Figure 4-3 SYMLOG Field Diagram

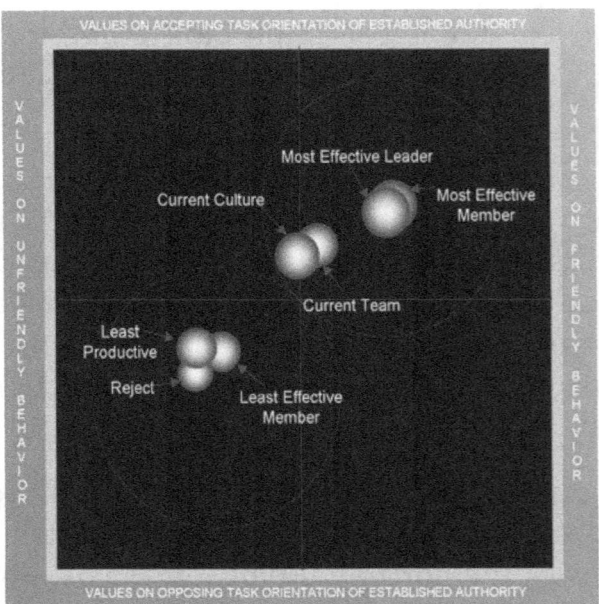

Aptitude and Skills Tools

The two sections above on personality and values instruments provide you with a sense of who you are. They can help you identify what is important in your career search but do not help identify what you CAN do in a career. An individual with a very extraverted personality who values team work may find that they are not well suited to outside sales because they simply do not possess the aptitude to understanding human behavior and closing techniques. Let's take a look at some of the tools available that can help you.

ASVAB – Armed Services Vocational Aptitude Battery

The ASVAB is an instrument with a VERY long history, proven reliability, and a wealth of information. As its name indicates, it is used by the Armed Services in the identification of specific aptitudes that potential members have in terms of occupational recommendations. Originally designed during World War I to help place new recruits in specific occupational fields, the ASVAB was known as the Army Alpha test. It was a series of written questions about skills and aptitudes. When it was determined that it was almost useless for its intended purpose due to the high level of illiteracy among the new soldiers and sailors, the Army Beta was developed which included pictures and was a much more successful instrument for its intended purpose. After several iterations, including the Army General Classification Test (AGCT) and the Navy General Classification Test during World War II, the ASVAB was developed and adopted for use by all services.

Today, the ASVAB is used by many organizations to determine the placement of candidates, the screening of candidates for specific jobs, and general testing abilities of college students.

The specific fields that the ASVAB tests include:

- General Sciences (GS)
- Arithmetic Reasoning (AR)
- Word Knowledge (WK)
- Paragraph Comprehension (PC)
- Math Knowledge (MK)
- Electronics Information (EI)
- Auto and Shop Information (AI)
- Mechanical Comprehension (MC)
- Assembling Objects (AO)

Through the various combinations of the above sub-tests, the aptitude of an individual can be measured and analyzed to determine the appropriateness of their entry into a specific occupational field. Additional information on the ASVAB can be found at http://official-asvab.com/index.htm.

Researching Potential Careers

So how do you learn about occupations and what people employed in those occupations do? Let's take a look at several resources.

One resource you will find with more information than you can possibly use in your search is the federal government. Between the U.S. Bureau of Labor Statistics for the number of people hired, salaries, geographic salary comparisons, and other data to research careers in general and the O*Net (Occupational Network), you'll find a great deal of information on virtually any and every occupation you can imagine. The good news is technology has enabled us to quickly sort through all of the available information to get to the data that is relevant and best fits our needs.

You can access the O*Net at:
http://www.onetcenter.org/.

Figure 4-4

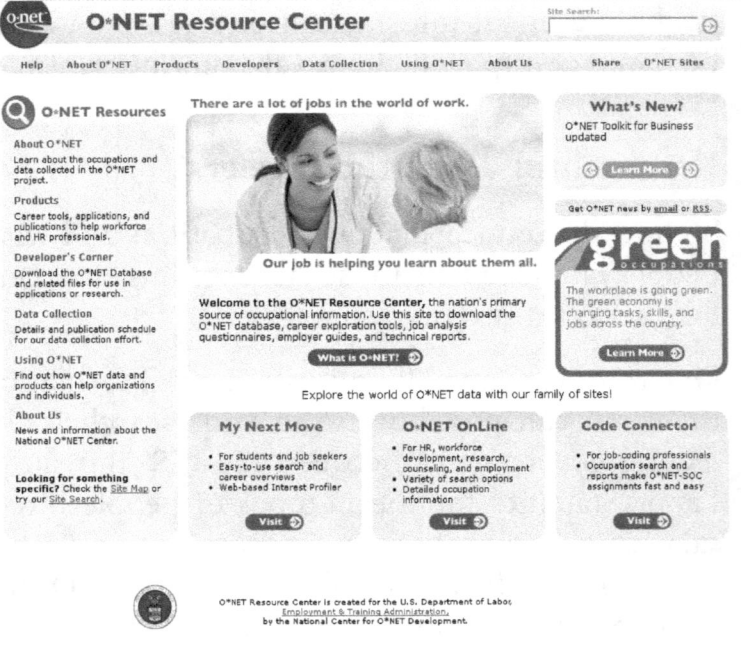

The U.S. Bureau of Labor Statistics also has a very good career resource entitled the BLS Occupational Career Outlook. The website is: http://www.bls.gov/oco/.

Not only will the U.S. Bureau of Labor Statistics' website provide the number of people in each occupation, but it also projects the need for those occupations into the future. It also has numerous other data sets that can be invaluable to you in preparing for your interviews on various industries and careers. This can be of immeasurable help if you are looking for a career that has excellent growth opportunity, need stability in your occupation, or are just willing to take a risk in an occupation that is of interest to you. It also provides the mean salary for individuals in that field.

Chapter 4 Summary

- There are many tests and instruments available to assist in your career search.
- Use the instrument that you find most suits your career goals.
- Do not use an aptitude test if you are trying to identify your personal values.
- View the results with a cautious eye. While many of these tools have been validated, there is always the possibility of an error.
- Seek assistance in interpreting the results if you do not understand them.

Chapter 4 Action Plan

Today: Find a free online career assessment tool and take it.

Tomorrow: Ask a friend or coworker if they find the same to be true about you as the assessment results indicate.

This week: Integrate the results into your job search toolkit.

Chapter 5
Your Toolbox of Career Search Success

In this chapter, we will be providing an overview of the functions of the various components of the Career Search System. In the following chapters, details on crafting each of these components will be discussed. The importance of understanding an overview of these items is to provide the perspective of alignment. Each component cannot stand on its own to achieve full functionality; it must be supported by each of the other components of the system. As you read the overview for each, you will be pleasantly surprised at how wonderfully they dovetail together to provide your potential employer and career field with a true picture of you, your abilities, and your potential.

We have already addressed the Career Search System component of research. This preparation is one of the most important aspects of your career fulfillment. The other components cannot succeed without your diligent efforts at finding the career that matches you and your personality, aptitude, skills, and desires. Creating the remainder of the components is a waste of time unless you have conducted the right amount of research.

Résumé

Many individuals spend a large amount of time, money, and effort in crafting their résumé, and rightly so. The résumé is your advertisement for your skills, abilities, and knowledge. The purpose of your résumé is to let employers know what you CAN do. Crafting and drafting your résumé comes with a responsibility for integrity and honesty, not only with yourself but also with the potential employers and hiring managers. Without an honest assessment of your past, your future will not look very bright. In addition to the non-published firings of many individuals who did not "quite tell the truth" on their résumés, there have been many recent newspaper stories of college coaches who misrepresented themselves.

The function of a résumé, in its various forms, is to get you the interview. It should provide enough factual information about you to qualify you for the position. Positioning your résumé in the marketplace and in the right hands of the potential hiring organization is one of the key strategies to the entire Career Search System. The résumé system currently in place by today's organizations can consist of a combination of technology and human eyes to determine whether a résumé has the minimum requirements for a candidate to fit a specific job description. Today's human resources offices can rapidly scan submitted résumés and cover letters for keywords and identify which résumés appear to fit the job description.

There are several types of résumés that are currently accepted and looked for in the workplace.

A **Universal Résumé** is pretty much what it claims to be—a résumé you can create, usually one or two pages in length, that can be used in a variety of situations and contains the majority of the experience and background you possess. The old theory that a one-page résumé is best is outdated. The correct length is the one that will provide the reader with the right amount of information.

An **Expanded Résumé** is one that is typically expanded beyond what you would initially send to a hiring manager. Typically brought during the initial interview with the hiring manager, it can point out the specific key skills you bring that address the needs of the organization.

A **Job Fair Résumé** provides you with a tool to use at job fairs. It will be given out to as many people as possible at a job fair, which includes other job searchers (which will be discussed in the networking section) in order to provide them with an overview of your key career direction and qualities.

An **Executive Biography** is used for those individuals at the upper management and leadership levels in organizations. Not only does it provide the reader with a sense of what they have done in the past, but it also provides them with a good picture of who they are. Typical executive biographies are 4-8 pages, depending on the previous career length of the job-searching executive.

In the early 2000s, one type of key résumé was an "electronic" résumé. This has become less evident in the job search environment with the advent of better document scanning tools and applications.

While this section has provided an overview of the function and purpose of a résumé, we will discuss the résumé in detail in the next chapter.

The Interview

As we discussed above, the purpose of a résumé is to get your qualifications in front of the hiring manager. It is the purpose of the résumé to show WHAT you can do. The purpose of the interview is for the organization to determine IF you will do the job for them. The interview is a crucial piece in the hiring process for both you, as a candidate, and the organization, as a potential employer. It is, in fact, a two-way communication tool, whereas the résumé is one-way. A hiring manager can look at a résumé all day long, but the facts on it will not change. The interview is a dynamic process that can provide hiring managers and coworkers with a great deal of information about who you are, what you have done, and what you CAN do.

Having a correctly aligned interview toolkit is very important to your success in the interviewing process. Your skill in interviewing can only come from practice. While this book and others can provide you with knowledge of the types of questions, what the questions are actually looking for, and how to best manage the interview, you will not be able to truly master this process and consequently put your best foot forward until you have practiced your interviewing skills.

The value of understanding and leveraging your experiences in the interview process can be improved through the use of our previous F*I*R*E model: Focus, Intensity, Relationship, and Execution.

FOCUS

Make sure you have cleared your mind of distractions. The interview, position, organization, and how you would fit into it should be front of mind. Thinking about or being distracted by irrelevant things like car maintenance schedules, children's report cards, and what to bring home for dinner should be avoided. On the other hand, you do not want to become so myopic and narrowly focused that you miss the larger scope of the interview questions or disregard the non-verbal communications of the interviewer. Focus includes being in tune with your own thoughts and feelings as well as being acutely aware of the environment around you.

INTENSITY

It is natural to become nervous when interviewing for a position. This is particularly true if you have not interviewed for a while or perhaps have not practiced enough. Similarly, you want to have some energy built up and want to be seen as enthusiastic. The interviewer knows you are likely to be nervous. They expect it. Having the appropriate level of intensity is important. Too high, and you come off as edgy, nervous, and anxious. Too little, and you come off as lethargic, slow, and unresponsive. You should monitor your level of intensity and align it to the level of interview, stage in the interviewing process, and intensity level of the interviewer. An effective strategy for intensity control in an interview is to show a high level of intensity at the beginning, reduce it slightly through the middle as you gain comfort with the questions and interviewer, then increase your intensity level again at the end to show enthusiasm.

RELATIONSHIP

While in the interview process, you are building relationships with each of the people you meet. Your relationship with those you meet is an ongoing and important maintenance consideration. I had a client who went to an interview with a hiring manager. They met for an hour and had a pleasant chat. My client thought it was "an OK interview. But I don't think I got the job." The next day, my client was having his car's oil changed at the local auto shop. While waiting in the lounge area, the hiring manager he had met with the day before came in. Rather than grilling him about the position and when a decision would be made or what his chances for getting hired were, my client took the opportunity to find out more about the organization itself and the hiring manager's experience there. Needless to say, this tactic provided the hiring manager with a much better picture of who my client was. The next week, a job offer was submitted, and my client was off and running in his new career.

EXECUTION

The execution of the interview process is where the rubber meets the road. You must be able to respond to the questions honestly, enthusiastically, and in a controlled manner. Remember that the interview process is a two-way communication tool. You are learning about the organization as they are learning about you. Take notes. Respond as you have practiced. The interview itself is not the time to try out new responses that you have not yet practiced. As we will discuss in the chapter on interviewing, there is a process called "soft control." Soft control provides you with the execution aspect of gathering information about the organization while also providing the organization with a very real picture of who you are and what you are capable of contributing to it.

In Chapter 11, we will be discussing the specifics of interviews. We will identify the types of interviews, the methods of gaining information from you, what you should do to gain information from the organization, and some methods for handling liabilities during the interview process. Interviewing is a skill that can and should be practiced and crafted so you feel comfortable answering questions and can think rapidly on your feet in responding to questions you may not have prepared for.

Compensation discussions and negotiations will be explored in Chapter 12. This chapter is where you determine your worth to the company and the company's worth to you. Negotiation techniques are varied. I have found the most effective compensation, and specifically salary, techniques are those that allow the organization to feel they are still in control, yet you know who is really controlling the situation. As we mentioned previously, "soft control" nets you the best package. A hard control or demanding approach will do little but alienate the very organization you want to partner with. At the same time, giving in to the minimal initial offerings the organization provides will leave you feeling resentful and dissatisfied. Not a great way to start off a career within a new organization.

The Evolving Career Search System

Each of the various components in your Career Search System contribute to an evolving progression of improvement. It should be a never-ending quest for improvement in each of your components. You should always try to be the one with a résumé ready when the word comes down that your organization is downsizing or another opportunity presents itself. YOU will not be the one they are referring to when they say, "Dust off your résumés, my friends. The time has come to move forward." Maintenance of your system is crucial to its ability to react, produce results for you, and be a source of pride.

Note now that I refer to the development of your Career Search System as an EVOLUTION and not a REVOLUTION. A revolution, like a car tire, typically has a starting point, rolls around and ends up with the spot on the tire a little further down the road, but it looks pretty much the same, while an evolution is a change process in which each event you work on, change, or even get rid of results in a change to and an improvement in the overall system. The linear evolution of your career is a change process that results in your career search tools becoming more evolved, better focused, and continuing to be ready to answer the challenges of your evolving career. Ultimately, when you need to change careers, which you will likely do at some point, your career search skills and toolbox will be that much better as the evolution moves you forward.

Chapter 5 Summary

- Tools and components of the career search system.

- The components must be used as they were intended.

- Each component supports the next one.

- The components in your Career Search System must be aligned with the appropriate amount of FIRE applied.

- Your Career Search System is an ever-changing one.

- The components in your Career Search System contribute to an EVOLUTIONARY system, NOT a revolutionary system.

Chapter 5 Action Plan

Today: Write 3 things you accomplished in past jobs in CARs format (this will be discussed in detail in the next chapter.)

Tomorrow: Write 3 MORE things you accomplished in past jobs in CARs format.

This week: Integrate the CARs into your résumé, interview preparation, and cover letters.

Chapter 6
The Résumé – Your Career Search centerpiece

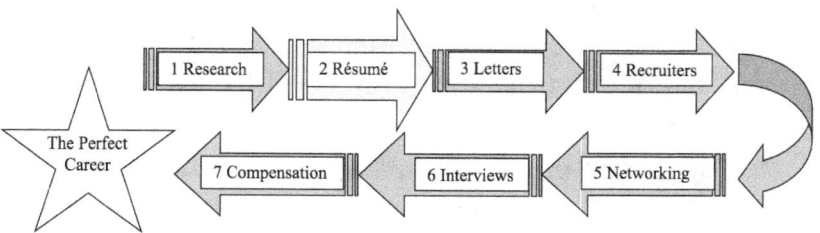

Your résumé is your work history. Employers need to know what you will contribute to the organization. During the screening phase of résumés, the only way they know what you can do is what you HAVE done in the past. In other words, the predictor of your future performance is your past performance. Not what your responsibilities were but what you DID!!! However, a résumé created in a vacuum without conducting adequate research on the industry, career path, and needs of the job is almost worse than not having any résumé out there at all.

The use of the résumé has changed over the past 30

years as a result of technology. Let's take a look at a typical search for an employee in 1980. The hiring manager identifies a need for a new front-line mechanic. He discusses this need with the human resources office that coordinates a job description with the hiring manager. The job description is developed from a "Job-Task" Analysis that identifies the key tasks the job requires. For a mechanic, these tasks might be diagnosing mechanical breakdowns, determining parts needed to repair, using the correct tools, estimating the time requirement to repair the breakdown, and testing the machinery. The HR manager and hiring manager then identify which tasks are most important to the job.

Once the job description is completed, the HR department sends out an advertisement to newspapers, trade journals, and perhaps the nearest university career center. Additionally, the hiring manager might also put the word out to his other mechanics that a new position is open.

Job applicants find the opening and send in their universal résumés and cover letters (to customize their qualifications) to the organization's HR department. Once the résumés start coming in to the HR department, it is up to them to screen the résumés to determine who may be the best fit from a qualifications perspective (education level, appearance—yes, sadly, HR did screen by how résumés looked—and years of experience.)

Then HR forwards the top 25-50% (depending on the number of résumés received) to the hiring manager, who continues the screening process. They typically selected 6 top applicants through an identification of the qualities they presented. They looked at their past history as to what they did, what they learned, and what they produced.

The purpose of the résumé is to provide a quick idea to organizations of your capabilities. Remember that it will not give the organization any sense of WHO you are, just what you can do. The important aspect of this is to include only information that the employer needs to determine IF you can do the job.

As we previously mentioned in Chapter 4, there are several different kinds of résumés for different purposes. The "Universal" résumé is one that you will typically use about 80% of the time. It provides the reader with a one or two page summary on your skills, abilities, and qualifications. The goal in your résumé is to let them know you CAN do the job. You have what it takes.

Long gone are the days when you could have one résumé and then simply prepare a cover letter to cover each of the various specific needs that a job posting might have. Today, you will likely prepare a separate and customized résumé for almost every job for which you apply. A lot of work? You bet.

Worth it? Also a resounding YES. So the trick is, how do you prepare a résumé that can fit the needs of various related job postings without having to totally rewrite your résumé each time? All part of the Career Search System.

Remember that the best predictor of your future potential is your past success. Clearly, you can't show ALL of your accomplishments in EVERY résumé, so the key is to develop some key entries that you can plug into your résumé each time you apply for a new job.

Lets take a look at the parts of a résumé. Clearly, we know you need a way to let the person in charge of a hiring or recruiting team get hold of you. So your name, address, email, and phone number go up at the top of the résumé. We will call this the "header." Remember that often you will be at a premium for space after you gain some experience. So you will want to maximize the space on your résumé. Can you see the difference in the two headers shown below?

```
Don Smith
222 Simpson Way * Bison, Wyoming * 82001 * (307) 555-1212 * dsmith@simpson.com
```

Or

```
Don Smith
222 Simpson Way          WASTED SPACE
Bison, WY 82001
(307) 555-1212
dsmith@simpson.com
```

You can see that in the second example, all the area to the right of the name and address is simply wasted space. Let's use all available space in our résumé to put information that the hiring manager can use to see what you CAN do. Whether your résumé is one page or two, wasted space is not going to endear you to hiring managers. Some résumé writers claim there is value to white space as it can bring out some important information. All of your information is important, and the time that a hiring manager has to read your résumé is limited, so maximize the use of their time by giving them the information they can use.

The Energy in Your Résumé

Imagine your résumé is a car. In this case, the car has an interchangeable engine that is easily replaced with one more suited for each trip you take. Going on a long trip? Want great gas economy? Plug in the smaller, more economical engine. Want to take her out to the drag strip? Put in the larger, more powerful engine. Want a luxurious ride? Put in the smoother engine.

So, where is this "engine" in your résumé? In fact, since the analogy works so well, we will call it CARs. It is a way to develop a catalog of your accomplishments.

Challenge – Identify the challenge you were faced with in your accomplishment.

Action – What was the action you took to resolve or improve the challenge?

Results – What were the results of the action you took?

Why CARs? Employers want to know that you can contribute to the success of their organization. They try to predict, based on the tools of the Career Search System, if you will behave in ways that are conducive to productivity. What is the best way to predict future behavior? Well since most crystal balls do not seem to work these days, they have to rely on your past behaviors to try to predict your future ones. This is why CARs is such an important piece of your overall Career Search System. It tells a story about what you did previously and how you were able to provide positive results.

Let's take a look at an example. Chuck was a new graduate with a Bachelor of Science degree in Business Administration. He had held several retail jobs during his time in college but really wanted to get a job as a marketer in the aerospace industry. When Chuck first came to me, his résumé was fairly typical and looked like this:

> Charles Andrews
>
> 123 Anystreet
>
> Madison, WI 53715
>
> candrews@gmail.com
>
> Objective: Position as a marketing specialist within the Aerospace industry where I can use my skills and abilities to help market aerospace technology.
>
> Education: Bachelor of Science, Graduated June 3, 2007, Wisconsin School of Aeronautical Marketing, 3.89 GPA
>
> Sports Place, Westmorland, WI – January 5, 2004 – June 7, 2004 – Responsible for cleaning up and putting supplies back on shelves.
>
> Wine and Stuff – Shorewood Hills, WI – July 31, 2004 – January 10, 2005 – Helped stock shelves and operate cash resister. Wrote advertisements for local paper.
>
> Magnation Worldwide – Greentree, WI – April 15, 2005 – August 31, 2005 – Call center operator assisting cell phone users with their phones and services.

Chuck was a bit distraught as his résumé was not getting him the phone calls he needed to interview for jobs in his desired career of aviation marketing. As I sat down with Chuck, we discussed the value of inserting some data points, removing specific dates, and overall providing a much more polished résumé that reduced his liabilities and highlighted his accomplishments more than his responsibilities. **Everyone has responsibilities at work, but it is the actual accomplishment of those responsibilities and how they are presented that REALLY interests the hiring manager.**

As a result of our work, Charles' résumé ended up looking like the one on the following page. Notice the differences between the two:

- Name and contact information fits into two lines

- Career "Objective" replaced with his "Position Statement," which includes the industries in which he wishes to work.

- Key skills are identified to maximize a fit with a job listing.

- Responsibilities have been replaced with CAR, identifying what he found out, what he did, and what the quantifiable results were.

- Dates were positioned so as to remove the glaring gaps in employment.

As an exercise, YOU decide which résumé would encourage you to call Charles in for an interview.

CHARLES ANDREWS
123 ANYSTREET * MADISON, WISCONSIN * 53715 * CANDREWS@GMAIL.COM * 608-555-1212

AVIATION MARKETING ASSOCIATE
AVIATION MAINTENANCE ADVERTISING/GENERAL AVIATION MARKETING/

CUSTOMER SERVICE REPRESENTATIVE

Key Skills

Organization	Customer Contact	Team Oriented
Leadership	Presenting Data	Analyzing Data
Knowledge of Aviation Industry	Excellent communicator	Detail oriented

Education

Bachelor of Science in Aerospace Marketing 2007,
Wisconsin School of Aeronautical Marketing, Graduated cum laude

Accomplishments

Inventory Control - Sports Place - Westmorland, WI – 2004

   As an inventory control specialist, identified key areas for improvement of inventory display. Rearranged inventory to provide logical presentation of equipment. This provided rapid inventory assessment, improved customer needs identification, and increased sales by approximately 20% over a 3-month time frame.

Marketing - Wine and Stuff – Shorewood Hills, WI – 2004 – 2005

   As sales point operator, analyzed customer flow and noticed competition had higher walk-in customer rate. Through customer inquiries, developed marketing plan for use in local advertising medium including online and periodicals. Resulted in approximately 24% increased customer walk-in rate and commensurate increase in overall sales.

Customer Relations - Magnation Worldwide – Greentree, WI 2005 –

   As sales point representative, noticed that typical calls were taking approximately 6.7 minutes to complete. Developed a script that would rapidly assist in identifying the key need of the customer and developed a logic tree to resolve customer concerns more rapidly. After piloting program, the business unit adopted the script and logic tree. Mean call time was reduced for the unit from 6.7 minutes to 4.2 minutes and customer "on hold" time by 45 seconds per incident.

Chapter 6 Summary

A résumé is a summary of your experience, training, and accomplishments that you have accumulated over your lifetime that will contribute to you successfully being able to complete the position for which you are applying. So when you prepare your résumé, you should be comparing what you are providing to the requirements for the position. If you put in too much information, you will be seen as overqualified. Too little or poor quality information, and you will be seen as not the best qualified. Either of these situations will NOT likely get you to the next step in the career process of interviewing with the decision makers. Again, the key we want to stress here is that your résumé must be aligned with the career you want, the experience you bring, the cover letter and other communication tools you use, and your ability to interview positively.

Chapter 6 Action Plan

Today: Identify the challenges in your current résumé.

Tomorrow: Find a job you would LOVE to have (even if you are not currently looking for a new job.)

This week: Rewrite your résumé for the job you identified, include key skills for the job listing, use CARs, and maximize the available space.

Chapter 7
Letters, Communications, Careers, and Control

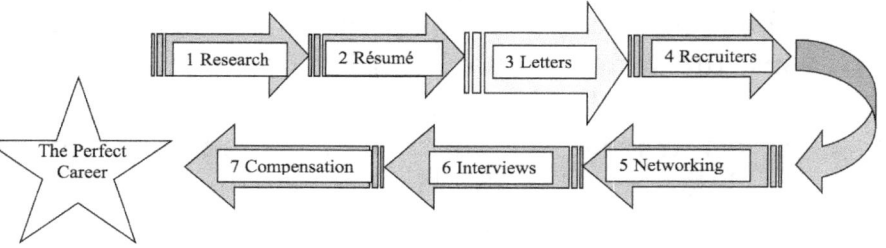

In years gone past, the résumé was seen as a relatively stable and unchanging job search tool that you used to apply for a multitude of jobs. You would then provide additional items that would help modify the résumé to show the company that you not only had the skills, knowledge, and abilities, but that you were a good fit for the position and organization as well. In today's world of word processing, computers, and the ability to search and replace words in a document at will, your résumé is expected to be a much better tool for showing an organization what you bring to the table and how you can contribute to the success of the organization. Does this mean that cover letters, telephone calls, and other supplementary documents are no longer necessary? Absolutely not.

Employers today consistently state that the number-one skill that shows them an individual can contribute to and fit within their organization is communication skills—in writing, speaking, attitude, and body language. Communication of your ability to fill a specific position is much more than just throwing a résumé at a job opening, hoping someone will see it and will call you because it meets their needs. Career search communication is about knowing the language of the company —understanding their needs and being able to provide them with a true perspective of what and who you are. They WANT to hire you, but they simply WON'T hire you if you do not fit. Showing how you fit the position is the job of the supplemental communication tools that you prepare for an opening in an organization.

Recently, I had the opportunity to sit in on the search committee of a private university. They were looking for a professor in a specific department. The job opening was posted nationwide in a large professional journal. The number of curriculum vitaes/CVs (a fancy term for a résumé used to find professors or other academic and scientific positions) submitted in response to the posting was unbelievable. We received more than 100 CVs within a two-week period. Sorting through these to get to the ten best we received was not difficult. Several clearly did not have the academic requirements, some had misspellings of the university name, and others were simply a smattering of everything the individual had done in their entire life dating back to elementary school. It was surprising that within a very short period of time, we were able to cull this pile of CVs down to the best 5. Why? They were brief, to the point, and reduced the candidates' liabilities while enhancing the assets of what they could bring specifically to the university and the position.

Why did we read the CVs that we did? Because the cover letters and opening emails were illustrative of the qualities we were looking for in finding the best fit for the position and organization. The others may have had more qualifications, better publications, and more prestigious backgrounds, but the information was never seen by the hiring managers.

The challenge for us as hiring managers, in this situation, was that we were left with the best CVs but not necessarily the best candidates. This is a clear example of how, even though you might BE the best candidate, the BEST material is what might get you the job. Spend your time where it will be best seen and best evaluated. Your résumé/CV has the largest amount of information about you for the hiring manager. However, if the cover letter does not grab their attention first, your résumé may never be seen.

Chapter 7 Summary

- Your résumé is a statement of your skills.

- Your résumé shows potential employers that you CAN do the job.

- Your résumé SHOULD be customized to each position for which you apply.

- Your résumé **will not** get you the job by itself.

- Supplement your résumé with solid supporting material that shows the potential hiring manager you WILL do the job.

Chapter 7 Action Plan

- Evaluate your current résumé for appropriate use of space, use of key words for your industry, and appropriate information for your CARs.

- Increase the number of CARs you have ready by at least 3. Remember, we want a library of accomplishments that are indicative of the productivity you have had in the past.

- Write a rough draft of a cover letter that you would use for the dream job you want,,then read it out loud. Does it sound like someone really wants to work there?

- Give the rough draft of a cover letter to a friend, and have them read it and give you feedback.

Chapter 8
The Recruiter – Friend or Foe?

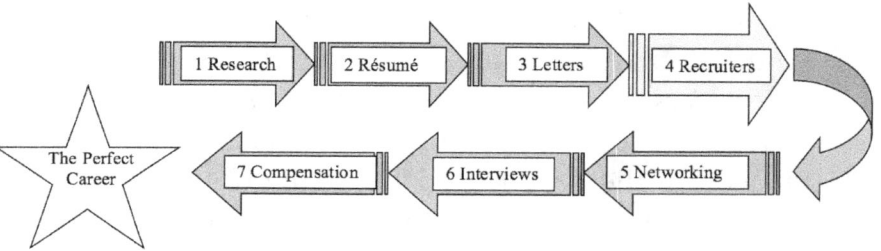

Ah, the recruiter! Most often when we think of the word, we think of the military model of a sharp dressed Soldier, Sailor, Airman, or Marine sitting behind a desk with a colorful picture of lands to be visited or foes to be conquered. Their job is to try to get as many candidates to the screening process as possible while providing a candidate with a good view of the armed forces.

Recruiters for companies are not too different. Recruiters will go out and try to get as many "pre-qualified" candidates as they can. The typical recruiter will try to get as many as 100 candidates for one job. Consequently, they are often also called "headhunters."

There are many different variations of recruiters. They can work for large national firms, or they can have their own "mom-and-pop shop." They can specialize in geographic areas, or they can have national clients. Some are very good at matching individuals to organizations and, as a result, have an excellent placement rate. Others are average, but still manage to make a living. You should ask recruiters about their placement statistics and success rates. How many individuals have they placed in the past year? How many of those were in the industry you are interested in? How many placements in that industry in their lifetime? If possible, ask to speak with other candidates they recently placed so you can hear, first hand, what those recruits' experiences were with the recruiter.

Remember that the recruiter will basically be selling you to the company, so it is in your best interest to treat your relationship with him or her as you would your potential boss. While it can pay to be honest with your recruiter, you should never be casual, sloppy, unkempt, or disorganized. Your recruiter will form an opinion of you, and he or she will pass on this opinion to the employer. Recruiters are always paying attention and are observant of even the smallest details. Many job searchers make the mistake of going to meetings with recruiters in casual clothes, thinking that it is not a "real" interview. Believe me when I tell you, this meeting is in fact a very real interview with incredible potential.

The recruiter is a positive tool in any job searcher's toolkit. But knowing how to work with them can reap benefits not only for one job but for many future potential jobs and opportunities as well. How does the typical recruiter function? Recruiters work for companies, NOT for job hunters. They get paid by the company they contract with when a position is filled through their efforts.

Some recruiters work for a specific company to hire individuals FOR that company, while other recruiters work for a search firm. Companies will often hire a search firm to help them find candidates for senior-level positions as a result of the networks they have formed.

Recruiters' fees are typically provided as a percentage of the annual salary of the position for which they are recruiting. Consequently, the more you earn, if placed by a recruiter, the more they will earn. So recruiters are generally motivated to ensure you are offered the best possible starting salary.

Recruiters typically become specialized in a specific industry. I have worked with recruiters who were VERY specialized in consultants, specifically Organization Development consultants. The good recruiters will be honest with you and let you know the probability of getting a specific salary.. Recruiters are an EXCELLENT source of information for specifics about potential jobs in key areas of the country and expected salaries.

So how can you maximize the skills and abilities of a recruiter? The following steps can help improve your experience when working with one:

- Establish a solid relationship. Take a recruiter to lunch.

- If you do not know of any recruiters in the field you are interested in, ask one in a related field if he or she knows of any they would recommend. They will often get a cut of the referral if the new recruiter places you, so they are open to this approach.

- Stay in touch with your recruiter, and send them holiday cards. Why? You want recruiters to remember YOU. A small gesture like this shows that YOU are considerate of them and their time.

- Send your recruiter career updates. If you are ever written up in a newspaper or trade bulletin, send them a clipping or an e-mail link to the item. Keep them updated on new skills you have acquired. One good way to do this is to invite your recruiter to your LinkedIn profile. Keeping them apprised of your career, skills, or accolades may help you stay front-of-mind when he or she is recruiting for an exceptional position in your field.

- Begin EVERY conversation with your recruiter with, "How are things?" This indicates you are interested in the field as well as their own well-being.

- Recruiters see a lot of résumés. Ask them for feedback on yours. Be open to making the changes they recommend for specific positions. Remember, they know what the organization is looking for and what skillset the ideal candidate possesses.

Chapter 8 Summary

- Understand the field you want to get into, and find a recruiter who specializes in that field.

- Use recruiters as an extended network of influence for companies.

- Don't be afraid to have more than one recruiter working for you.

- Ask recruiters about the hot career sectors in your field. Often, companies have a tough time finding key people in these areas. This is an opportunity for you to get into a new area early.

Chapter 8 Action Plan

- Find 3 to 5 recruiters in your area, and then Google them for reviews on their performance.

- Request a meeting with a recruiter to review your résumé, and evaluate it compared with what they have seen.

- Contact someone who is currently working in your field or for a company related to your field, and ask them if they are aware of any industry specific recruiters that have an excellent reputation.

CHAPTER 9
Use the Web – Technology for all of Us

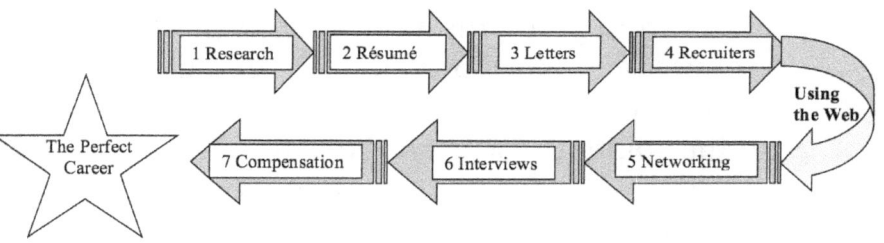

Over the past 20 years, the Internet has become an indispensable part of our lives. We surf the Internet. We shop on the Internet. We maintain contact on the Internet. We use the Internet to obtain information to help us make decisions. Recently, we have seen the advent of the term Web 2.0. If we recall, the Internet was used as an informational resource for the first few years. We could use the Internet to obtain information and contact friends. In the years since about 2004, the Internet has become more of a two-way avenue for us to not only obtain information but also to put out information about us. The growth of YouTube, Facebook, Twitter, LinkedIn and other social media sites, online classes, and many other tools have enabled us to do many things virtually that we could not before.

In the 1980s and 1990s, working from home was something you only did if you had no other options. Today, many organizations are leveraging the virtual environment to reduce their carbon footprint in their office spaces, allowing employees to work from home and yet still be as productive, in some cases MORE productive than if they were at work. Reduced distractions, creative resources, and the ability to focus on the task at hand without fellow employees' interruptions have enabled many people to work directly out of their homes.

The Internet has also been an invaluable resource for career searchers. It allows us to put our skill sets out to many potential employers very quickly. It helps us research current trends in the career fields we would like to enter. It provides us with the ability to contact employers and hiring managers very quickly.

But if the Internet does all this for us, why do we not find ourselves flooded with job offers? The answer is of course that those same employers are being flooded with applications, emails, résumés, and job information requests from all of the other job searchers as well. The key is to differentiate YOUR information from that of the other 99% of job searchers doing the same thing.

In Richard Bolles' outstanding book on career search *What Color Is Your Parachute*, he relates to the story of an Army Captain who was looking for employment after leaving the Army at the completion of his obligation. After 6 years in the Army, he had accumulated quite a few skills in directing artillery, motivating soldiers to march and dress smartly, and working with other countries' military forces. Unfortunately, there was not much in the way of need for someone with those specific skills. He decided to differentiate his cover letter to potential employers by posting a picture of himself on an old tractor with a caption about his ability to sell. What did his ability to sell an old tractor have to do with his skill set? Not a whole bunch, but he received a lot of phone calls for interviews.

Now, I'm not advocating that you put funny pictures on all of your job search materials. In fact, most organizations will automatically disqualify you for a potential position if a picture is present to avoid any potential discrimination accusations. But the point is that in order to stand out and get noticed, you need to make sure that your materials show that you ARE different from the other candidates—different in a BETTER way. What are employers looking for? First and foremost, above all, employers are looking for integrity.

Using the Internet for your job search can be frustrating if not managed correctly. Keep records of your searches. When you receive an acknowledgement, make sure you track when, how long it took to get feedback, and what the source was for that job lead. If you cannot replicate your successes, chances are you WILL replicate your failures. Keeping track of both gives you the opportunity to see what works and what does not and to adjust accordingly.

There are many helpful job searching websites out there that you can easily get lost in. As of September 2015, the top job search engine was Craigslist with 51.3 million unique visitors (http://www.listofsearchengines.info/job-search-engines). Here are a few others listed below:

2. Indeed.com

3. TheLadders.com

4. Monster.com

5. Careerbuilder.com

6. Simplyhired.com

7. Dice.com

8. Mediabistro.com

9. Snagajob.com

10. Salary.com

11. Beyond.com

When you use these websites, with the possible exception of Craigslist.org, you will set up an account and a job agent. A job agent is simply the criteria and types of positions you want the site to search for you. It will then go out and search its database for jobs matching the criteria you selected. All too often, individuals use terms that are specific to their only historical job or place, with so many different parameters around the job that nothing comes up. One example might be:

Type of job: Cereal Tester

Location: Mojave, California

Salary desired: $50,000

Availability: Monday, Wednesday, Friday, 8-10 a.m.

Travel: NO

Clearly this is an exaggeration, but you get the idea. Provide broad terms that will help find enough jobs to give you a direction and provide some optimal chances of success.

You can also have more than one job agent per website, and most of the job search sites encourage this. You might have one for your primary dream position but then draft up three or four others for positions that would also be acceptable to you.

Chapter 9 Summary

- The technology and use of the Internet can be a wonderful tool, but it must be managed.

- Use the online recruiting tools, but make sure that your information is consistent.

- Be aware that many people are using these same tools. Make your resume and application stand out by using key words in your field.

- Set up multiple agents to search in different areas.

Chapter 9 Action Plan

Today: Visit the career search sites provided, and create a profile for at least 5 sites. Identify and prioritize the criteria for your job ideas, and come up with several key words for each.

Tomorrow: Develop at least 3 search agents for each of the sites you have signed up for.

One month from now: Review the search agents, and modify them accordingly.

CHAPTER 10
Networking

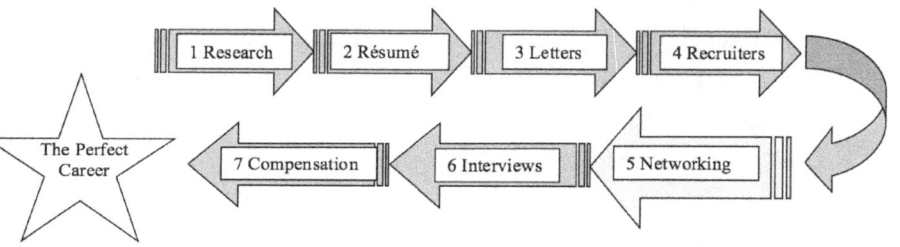

Jill was at the "Mid-Sized Trademark" tire store getting her oil changed one Wednesday morning. As she sat and waited for her car to get finished, she noticed a well-dressed woman, apparently also waiting for her car, reading a book that Jill had just finished on leadership. "Great book," Jill offered.

"So far, I've found it totally engaging," responded Elisa. "I have often admired leaders who can quickly obtain results while not burning out their people." Jill related a short story about her leadership experience to Elisa. When Elisa asked, "Where do you work?" Jill responded that she was in between jobs, having just been laid off as a result of downsizing from a large pharmaceutical company. The conversation continued, and at the end of it, after exchanging business cards, Elisa asked Jill to send her a résumé for her to review. Within two weeks, Jill interviewed with Elisa's company and found a position perfectly suited to her lifestyle and skills.

While this may not happen every day, you should be aware of the opportunities as they present themselves. This also means being willing to open yourself up to options other than your dream job. Some professions need leaders and managers with higher-level skills than the lower-level positions and do not rely only on internal candidates. Stretch yourself, and you will be surprised at what can happen.

It has been estimated that fewer than 5% of all successful job and career searches are the result of finding jobs on the Internet or in the newspaper. So, where is that other 95%? It is all done through networking. You might know someone who got a job by knowing someone who knows someone. Networking. Or a friend of yours might tell you there is an open position at his place of work. Networking. Or, as a result of an informational interview, a rival company to the one at which you interviewed calls you up because the boss mentioned you were a good candidate but just did not have an opening. Networking. Or you may have attended a professional association such as the Society for Human Resources, American Society for Training and Development, Organization Development Network, or another association, and they remembered you. You guessed it ... networking. Even when you are employed and not looking for work, you may find out that your network is looking for opportunities for you. And of course there are the current technology enhanced networking tools such as Facebook, Google+, LinkedIn, and Twitter—all excellent tools to let as many people as possible, in the right positions, know what you want to do.

So how do we leverage networking to make it work the best for us? What is the secret to energizing this magical career search tool that has netted so many careers for others? The key is "strategic networking." Is it possible to do too much networking? Not likely. Even in the event you find a job and your network is still working for you, you will have other opportunities for success in addition to your current job. Community involvement, speaking engagements, and other opportunities are still going to be important to your career success. Let's take a look at some of the various networking strategies that are out there.

Informational Interviews

Informational interviews have been around a very long time. This is basically when you interview someone in the position you would like to have and find out what it takes to get there. The idea is not only to get the information from the interviewee but to also let them know you are interested in their work and what you are capable of doing. This avenue of interviewing is very successful but must also be tracked, and notes must be taken. The steps to informational interviewing are:

> 1. Contact a person of interest in the field in which you want to find a career.
>
>> a. Check the Yellow Pages either electronically or the hard copy.
>>
>> b. Check professional associations.
>>
>> c. Ask the chamber of commerce.
>
> 2. Ask them if they have the time to meet for an hour or so. Lunches work great; everyone has to eat.
>
> 3. Ask them about themselves. If they perceive you are only using them, you will not get as much information. You can ask, "How did YOU find this career attractive?" rather than, "What makes this an attractive career?"
>
> 4. Offer admiration for their achievements and accomplishments, and ask them to tell you a story about one. People love to tell stories.

5. Listen attentively, and jot down notes.

6. No matter what other questions you ask, you should end the conversation with, "Do you know of anyone else in the field who I may contact to ask about their experiences?"

7. Follow up with a thank you card, NOT AN EMAIL. People will remember your "Thank You" card much longer. Emails also have a tendency to get lost. You can put a card on your desk and see it for a long time. An email is looked at and then gone from our attention.

Social networking is a recent phenomenon that is helping many career and job searchers. Networking by itself is the number-one way to land a job. The use of technology can make this task even quicker and with better results. Using a variety of the social networking sites, whether Facebook, LinkedIn, Twitter, Google+, or others, you can reach out and let literally thousands of people know that you are looking for work in a specific area and have specific skills. This requires some additional word-crafting skills to ensure that your skills are highlighted and matched to the correct industry. In some cases, social networking via the web results in very quick replies or inquiries from recruiters looking to fill positions. Often, individuals may find that organizations are willing to hire them even before they have left their current organization.

Social Networking

Social networking can be a great deal of fun. You can make many connections quickly and connect back up with your old pals, but it also brings challenges of its own. How much information about you is too much information? If you currently have a Facebook, LinkedIn, Google+, Twitter, or other social media account, be careful about what you put out there. Many organizations today will do a simple Google search to learn more about you before deciding whether or not to pursue you as a candidate. If you have not done one lately, it pays to keep up on what the Internet has to say about you. Be careful about what pictures you post as well. A picture of you having a great time with a beer in your hand on vacation is a great conversation starter with your friends, but do you want that to be the first impression a potential employer has of you?

This is actually a very serious issue. There is a separate issue in which potential employers ask for your Facebook login to see what you have on your account. This is very controversial and in fact may be illegal in some cases. However, discretion is the better part of valor, and if you are job-hunting, you may wish to close your Facebook account if there is any possibility it could be used against you.

One strategy that some career searchers use is having two separate social media accounts—two separate identities for two distinct purposes: a professional one and a personal one. Not a bad idea if you can remember to update and maintain your professional one. It then becomes similar to a website that can market you and your specific skill set.

One of the most effective methods of networking is to attend job fairs. A job fair is a convention of sorts in which many organizations have a representative on hand answering questions and collecting résumés for potential employees. The value of job fairs is that you get to see many organizations and the people in them in a very short period of time. However, there are a few hints that can make the job fair more valuable than would at first seem evident.

- Do not just drop off your résumé at a company's booth and leave. Engage the representative from the organization. Ask them how they like working there. Look for things that tell you about the company such as their brochures, the support materials they have provided the representative, and the way that the representative is dressed. Use it as an informational interview.

- Talk to other job searchers at the job fair. Often, they might have heard of a company not at the fair that has openings. They might also be a company representative just taking a look around the fair to see what their competition is. Ask questions and exchange business cards. If you are between jobs, it is wise to have some personal "calling cards" available. Vista Print offers affordable business cards and regular discount offers. Be sure to include your name, phone number and email address.

- Craft a "Job Fair Résumé" that allows for you to write notes in the margin about yourself. This is sort of an informal cover letter that can make a big impression to potential hiring managers.

- Ask for additional contacts within the company. The representative will likely know the personalities of the individuals within the organization and can steer you to the right one.

Overall, the value of networking cannot be overstated. I would estimate that of all the individuals I have worked with in obtaining fulfilling careers, networking has helped find about 90% of the jobs. It is a skill that needs to be developed, not only for your career search but also for your career development once you find a solid position.

Finally, utilize your alumni resources for both your undergraduate and even high school networks. Keeping in touch with professors and former classmates is possible with social media and with real-time visits and involvement. Getting involved with the alumni group of your alma mater can also provide valuable networking opportunities.

Chapter 10 Summary

Networking CAN be the greatest asset to your career search, but it must be managed. Knowing the appropriate network for YOUR career dreams is important so that you can quickly target the location of your information and control its dissemination.

- Use professional associations.

- Volunteer for community projects.

- Proactively manage your social networking sites on the Internet. Changing your profile 2-3 times a week is NOT too often to make sure it is fresh and shows up correctly.

- Be aware of opportunities that arise through chance meetings with others.

Chapter 10 Action Plan

Consider a job or field that interests you. Identify an individual with whom you can schedule an informational interview to gather more information.

Contact your alumni group. Write 3 letters a week to people with whom you considered positive influencers in your network when in college or high school.

Attend a local Rotary Club or Chamber of Commerce mixer to make community connections.

Identify 5 professional associations in your area of expertise or profession. Review their website for conferences near you and plan to attend one per quarter (even AFTER you find your dream job.)

Chapter 11
The Interview

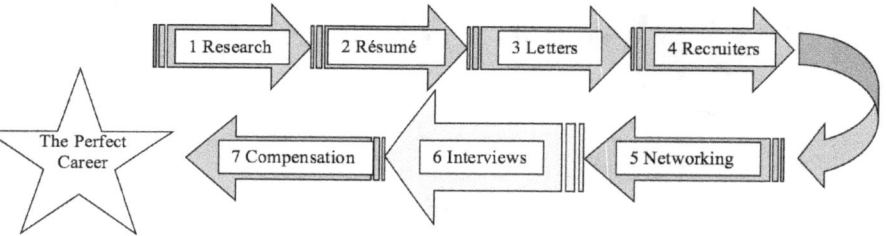

The interview! Few parts of the career search will cause this much anxiety and trepidation. "What if I say something wrong?" "What if they don't like me?" These are typical questions asked by nervous interview candidates. Should you be a bit nervous? ABSOLUTELY! It is a form of public speaking which has been acknowledged as the number-one fear of most Americans, exceeding even death. We all get butterflies during public speaking and interviews; however, the key to a successful interview is not to get rid of the butterflies, but to get them to fly in formation. Use the nervous energy you are developing, and show it as enthusiasm.

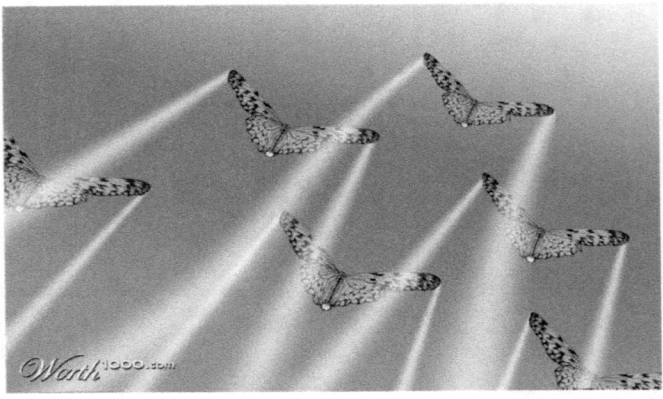

Believe it or not, the interviewer is also likely to be nervous. They, too, have much at stake in the employment interview.

How do you make the interview a positive aspect of your application? Your job during the employment interview is to find out what the employer is looking for in the perfect candidate. Whether it is a new position, someone has left the organization, or they simply need another employee, there is a reason they have an opening. Once you find the reason they are hiring, you can align your interview responses to meet their needs. Clearly, the sooner you can nail it down, the better. If you do not learn why the position is available until the end of the interview, all opportunities to answer questions that highlight your qualifications for their specific needs may be lost. It is often acceptable to ask the reason for the opening early in the process.

In all interview processes, it is important to remember from our discussion on resumés that the best predictor of your future capabilities is your past behavior. The potential hiring manager has nothing else to go on other than your past performance. It is up to you to bring it to light. Just as we discussed in the resumé section, using the CAR method can provide a very real picture of your past accomplishments and bring your real potential to light for the interviewer.

Challenge – What challenges did you face in your past job?

Action – As a result of the challenge, what action did you take?

Results – As a result of the action you took, how was the organization better off?

Using Soft Control

After all of your hard work researching, applying for positions via online applications, and sending out hard copy and electronic resumés, the call you have been waiting for has finally arrived. The phone rings, and the conversation goes something like this:

YOU: "Hello?"

VOICE ON PHONE: "Have I reached Jaime McConnahay?"

YOU: "Yes."

VOICE: "This is Acme Car Parts. We received your résumé and would like to schedule an interview."

YOU: "WONDERFUL! Yes, I'd be very happy to interview. When do you need me?"

VOICE: "We'd like to conduct an initial phone interview this Friday at 3:30 p.m."

YOU: Thinks, *Oh no, I am flying to meet my uncle in Chicago at 2pm on Friday,* but responds, "Yes, I can make it."

So, what has just happened here? Basically, You have lost control of your job search and are at the mercy of the phone. You have sacrificed control to your enthusiasm. When receiving calls for interviews, it is a bit better to maintain soft control. Instead of being overly excited and agreeing to all requests for an interview, take a deep breath. While it is clearly an exciting time and a move in the right direction, you still want to maintain a semblance of control over your career and job search. A better tactic would be to respond as follows after the phone rings:

YOU: "Good morning."

VOICE ON PHONE: "Have I reached Jaime McConnahay?"

YOU: "Yes, may I ask who's calling?"

VOICE: "This is Sue Williams, at Acme Car Parts. We received your résumé and would like to see if you're interested in conducting a telephone interview."

YOU: "That would be great! May I ask how you obtained my résumé?"

SUE: "We received it via a recruiter based in Phoenix. Would Friday at 3:30 pm work?"

YOU: "Actually, that wouldn't be a very good time for me. May I check my schedule and get back to you? May I have your phone number?"

SUE: "Certainly, it's 555-222-1111."

What we have done in this initial phase of the interview is maintained a soft control over the situation. Compared to "hard control," which often shuts down communications early in the process, we want to control the information flow so that it is indeed a two-way process. If you were to take "hard control," throwing question after question at the interviewer, you would come across as pushy, arrogant, and intolerable. But soft control shows interest, an ability to think on your feet, and consideration for the fit. We do not jump up and down and shout for glee, but we do show interest.

Now, not only do we have the opportunity to try to schedule the interview at a good time for us, but we also have a contact phone number within the organization that we can use to obtain additional information.

When you call back, within 15 minutes, the conversation might go something like:

SUE: "Acme Auto, Sue speaking."

YOU: "Hi Sue, Jaime McConnahay here. You called a few minutes ago regarding setting up an interview."

SUE: "Yes, Jaime, what did you find out?"

YOU: "I have an opportunity on Friday at 9 a.m., the following Monday at 10, or Tuesday in the morning. Would that work for you?"

SUE: "I see Mr. Witman has an opening on Tuesday at 10:30. Why don't I set you up then? Can I have him call you at this number? "

YOU: "That would be wonderful. I'll be here. May I ask how long the interview might take?"

SUE: "They typically take between 30 minutes to an hour."

YOU: "Wonderful. Do you know if Mr. Witman is the hiring manager?"

SUE: "Yes, he is."

YOU: "Excellent. Sue, thank you so much for your help. I look forward to meeting you in the near future."

Notice that during this exchange, the candidate asked questions after responding to the questions of the caller. This is very important to remember during each and every interview you attend. Soft control, through asking questions, is not only a wonderful way to show that you are interested and engaged, but it also gives you the opportunity to gain additional insight and information into the organization. Remember that the interview process goes both ways—the company is assessing your willingness to do the job, and you are evaluating the company's culture and fit with your personality.

As we discussed in chapter 7, the résumé is your opportunity to give the prospective employer the fact that you CAN do the job. The function of the interview is to determine if you WILL do the job. Résumés provide potential employers with facts, while the interview provides the employer with feelings.

In years gone past, there was often just one interview with the hiring manager. Today, it is not surprising to hear of an entry-level position candidate experience 2 or 3 interviews, and the higher you go, the more interviews you can expect.

One of my clients applied for a Senior Trainer position at FedEx. He had actually found the job through networking. The position had just posted the day before he called the hiring manager and submitted the application. FedEx HR conducted a phone interview to verify the information on the application and résumé. The next day, the hiring manager and the Director of Training Services called and set up an appointment to come in for a mock training, during which he was asked to provide a brief 15-minute training on a topic of his choice.

Several days after that, he was asked to come in

and interview for an hour with the hiring manager. The following week, my client went back to FedEx headquarters and conducted 4 short individual interviews with potential coworkers.

The irony of this story is that after all this time and money spent on the interviewing process, while waiting for a response to the application, my client found a different job with a competitor. Out of curiosity, he called FedEx a week later to find out about the position. The position had not been filled and had actually been canceled due to a new departmental policy on an increased use of computer-based training. However, it was wonderful practice for my client, and since he had left FedEx on a positive note, he would still be able to use FedEx as an additional networking tool in the future.

Categories of Employment Interview Questions

The categories of interview questions are those styles used by the interviewers to get as much information about you to fit the position as possible. The types of questions should be aligned with the position for which you are interviewing. Unpracticed interviewers may default to a generalized discussion, but do not be caught off guard; savvy interviewers will simply begin talking to you, keying in on specific words, experiences, and your background to explore your fit within the organization. Even though some interviews may not seem like interviews, you are being observed, and your behaviors (including body language), as much as your words, will tell the interviewer much about you and your fit within the organization.

You can expect the following interviews initiated by employers as a result of your career search:

Initial Phone Call Interview

Conducted to ensure you are available and to set up your follow-up interviews. Typically an early screening type of phone call is to make sure you're a real person and to evaluate your personality as well as your interest in the position. Sometimes, if you are applying for a position in another geographic location, this might be a screening call by a hiring manager to see if they want to go through the expense of bringing you in for a full set of interviews.

One-on-one Interview

These face-to-face interviews are often conducted by a hiring manager to confirm the information on your résumé and to explore your experience and interest in the potential position.

Panel Interview

Sometimes conducted via telephone and often during on-site interviews. This gives the opportunity for the panel members to observe your responses to others while not having to actually think about the content. During this interview, the panel members will typically ask focused and specific questions assigned to them. During higher-level position openings, the panel interview may take place during a lunch or dinner. They are observing everything you do. While not very common, the possibility exists that you may be in a panel interview with several panel members while they are conducting interviews with several candidates at the same time. In other cases, you may be called into a panel interview in which each member of the panel is actually a hiring manager for a position in his or her department. Always be ready to provide answers to a variety of specific questions in generalizable ways, and include examples of how you might handle or have handled situations.

(These are actually quite difficult and can really throw applicants for a loop. A panel of seven interviewed my daughter when she applied to work at an Apple retail store. Her ability to remain calm and not get frazzled allowed her to pass through to the next round of interviewing. Apple only hires 7% of its applicants, so they purposefully try to make the process difficult and somewhat off-putting.)

Coworker Interview

This interview, conducted by potential coworkers and sometimes even individuals who may work for you if applying for a leadership position, is often done to see how well you will fit with their team. Many organizations will have potential coworkers take candidates to lunch. While the setting may seem relaxed or casual, remember that your words and actions are being scrutinized. Typical questions you might hear are: "So what do you think of the company so far?" or "How has your day been going?" Use this opportunity to talk about what you like about the company, department or team. Remember, in addition to learning about your skills and experience, potential coworkers are also trying to determine whether your personality will fit within the team dynamic.

Styles of Interview Questions

In addition to the above-mentioned types of interviews, there are several styles of questions that have been accepted as beneficial in understanding the personality and fit of the candidate. These question styles are:

Structured Questions

These questions are asked exactly the same for every candidate. The responses are recorded, and then the next question is asked. There is no room for creativity or follow-up in structured interviewing. Typically, structured interview questions are asked either by HR or during the very first interview if there is to be a series of interviews. They may be questions such as: "Do you have experience in working with customers over the phone?" or "Can you operate a computer?" Usually closed-end, these are good questions for rapidly finding out about the capabilities of the candidate. The disadvantage is it does not give the interviewer the freedom to dig a bit deeper into your responses. In the structured interview, the interviewer is looking for the content of the answer rather than the way you answer the question. Short responses are best used when responding to structured interview questions unless there is a weakness in your answer. One example might be if you are applying for a position that requires a Bachelor's Degree in Business Management but you have 8 years of experience and no degree. Then you would want to provide the rationale for the "no" answer.

In structured interviews, there is often little room for you to ask a question at the end of your response. Save your questions until the end of this particular style of interview. Structured interviews might be used for a variety of reasons, the most prevalent being that the organization has a time limit and needs to get through many initial candidates. Do not take these interviews lightly, and answer the questions as fully as possible. Know how to read the interviewer. If they look impatient, you should probably shorten your answers. If they continue to maintain eye contact after you respond, elaborate on your answer. In some structured interviews, you may be asked to move on to the next question. Do not take this as a sign that you did not answer correctly. Remember, this style of interview is frequently used because time is limited, and you simply may have already answered the questions sufficiently.

Semi-Structured Interview Questions

The semi-structured interview question provides the interviewer with the opportunity to follow up on any questions that might provide insight into the fit and alignment of the candidate's personality and abilities with the needs of the position. Going back to our previous question of "Do you have experience working with customers over the phone?" while you might answer with, "Yes," the interviewer can then go a bit deeper into the question with, "Tell me a little more about your abilities to work with customers over the phone." The semi-structured interview provides a platform for exploring those needed areas a bit deeper while still completing the overall focus of the interview and finding out the minimum necessary answers to the questions. As a candidate, you want to make sure that you answer the questions completely and highlight your assets while not discussing any potential liabilities.

Behavioral Interview Questions

Behavioral interview questions are those questions that ask you to provide an example of how you acted previously in a specific situation. Preparing for behavioral interview questions requires being confident and transmitting the confidence to the interviewer through your response. Some sample behavioral questions that have recently been popular are:

- Can you provide me with an example of a time when you knew you were correct and your supervisor was incorrect? How did you handle this situation?

- Tell me about a time when you had to decide whether to agree with the customer or decide to protect the organization you worked for.

- Tell me about a time when you were under a very tight timeline.

As you can see, there are really no right or wrong answers to these questions. They are dependent upon your ability to quickly identify a previous situation and discuss your thought process as you worked through it. It is also quite evident that the above questions can readily be asked of anyone as they are common workplace occurrences.

You might also see that each of these questions is ideal for you to use CARs. From your library of CARs, you can identify one that fits and discuss it in this situation. As an example for the final question, "Tell me about a time when you were under a very tight timeline," you can respond with, *"(CHALLENGE) In one of my recent positions as a parts manager for an auto dealership, we received word on a Friday afternoon that one of the shipments of parts we received had several defective parts in it. (ACTION) I quickly decided to return the entire shipment rather than take a chance on some of the defective parts remaining in the system. Since we had already installed several of the parts on customers' cars, we needed to rapidly contact them and have them return to us for free replacements. I explained to my team the urgency in this matter. (RESULTS) We were able to replace and reinstall that same afternoon all 10 of the client's parts that had been previously installed. We held a debrief afterwards to discuss what we could have done better as well as what we did that was strong. (SOFT CONTROL) Do you find that sometimes your organization also has these types of situations?"*

Here you can see that the CARs method actually

provides the platform for the response to the behavioral question.

Behavioral questions are your opportunity to provide examples of your successes in the past. You should relate them in a confident tone while maintaining eye contact with the interviewer.

Situational Interview Questions

In situational interviewing, a hypothetical situation is generated, and the interviewer is looking for your reaction as well as your thought processes when responding. An example might be, "What would you do if you saw one of your fellow coworkers loading a computer monitor into his or her car after working hours in the parking lot of their workplace?" In this case, the interviewer is not only looking for your answer, but HOW you answer. The key is to develop a process that helps you identify the correct way to behave in that situation. If your response is a flat, "I'd turn them in," that tells the interviewer one thing about you. You can respond with a more thoughtful, *"(CHALLENGE) If I saw a fellow coworker loading a computer monitor into their car after work, I would have to ask myself why they might be doing that. (ACTION) I would probably observe their behavior, and if I suspected something was wrong, I might go up and ask them some questions about what they were doing. (RESULT) Once I receive the answer, I'd follow up with their supervisor just to ensure it had been cleared."* This tells them more about your thought processes and how you work through problems.

Again, the situational question is ripe for the use of CARs when responding. It provides you with a solid set of guidelines within which you can frame your response and provide your processes in the response as well. Notice that, in this situation, we did not ask a question as it was a hypothetical situation.

How to Manage "Liabilities" During the Interview

Sometime during your interviews there will come a time when the interviewer asks you a question in which you find yourself discussing a negative aspect of your career or lack of a specific qualification. There are several strategies for these types of questions. We will review a few of the most prevalent types here.

The "Iceberg" Technique

The "Iceberg" technique is typically used when there is an issue that appears on your résumé that the interviewer has a specific question about. If you consider the typical iceberg, about 90% of it is not visible. With only 10% above water, an iceberg is really a large problem, but you only see a small portion. Similarly, this technique only provides them with a small portion of the actual liability. This liability could be lack of a specific qualification, a gap in your employment history, or about a job you recently left under less-than-ideal circumstances. This technique requires that you respond, in a brief manner, about the incident and do NOT expand on it. Only provide the "tip of the iceberg" to the problem. A good example might be if the interviewer notes, "I see you have a gap in employment of about 6 months. Can you tell me a bit about what you were doing during that time?" In this case, you might simply state, "I had a consulting opportunity." Do not elaborate and say what the opportunity was or how it turned out. If the interviewer wants to know more about it, they will ask.

Redirection strategy

Another strategy that can work when addressing your liabilities, either uncovered during the interview process or revealed in your résumé, is to turn the liability into an asset. This particular technique really takes quite a bit of practice. An interviewer may note that you have experience in an industry that is different from the one the potential hiring organization is in. In this case, you can try to get to the actual crux of their concern by requesting clarification. "I think that what you are really asking is if you think I can do the job in a new industry. Am I correct?" Once the interviewer confirms that is actually what they need to know, you can provide a CARs that shows that you are adaptable and can learn quickly. Again, the question at the end of your response provides the "soft control" you need to get the interviewer to provide additional information.

The interview is your opportunity to show you have the will and skill that the company needs. The key is to find out early exactly what the organization needs and then adjust your responses to show that you can fill that gap. All too often, individuals who would be GREAT employees for an organization simply fail to show that they are the right person to fill in the gap that the company has. It is not always the BEST person who gets the job; it is the person who has the RIGHT responses based on the needs of the organization. Practice your interviewing techniques to maximize your ability to gain information about the needs of the organization.

Remember, it's not always the BEST QUALIFIED person who gets the job; it's the one who fits the organization's hiring NEEDS the best.

Chapter 11 Summary

The interview is a crucial component in your armory of career search tools. You need to make sure that it is in agreement with your résumé and that your interviewing skills are honed. There are standard sets of questions all candidates must be ready to answer, but be ready for the odd questions that may be thrown in. Interviewing is a skill that, like driving and cooking, can be developed with practice. As in any information exchange in which there will be a transaction, the better prepared you are, the better your chances of landing that dream job. RESEARCH, RESEARCH, RESEARCH.

Chapter 11 Action Plan

Today: Write out your answers to the top five interview questions:

1. Tell us about yourself
2. Why should we hire you?
3. What are your strengths?
4. What are your weaknesses?
5. What do we get when we hire you?

Tomorrow: Practice your responses with a friend to make sure they are authentic and genuine and will finish up with a question.

This week: Videotape yourself answering these questions and analyze yourself from an employer's perspective…would YOU hire YOU with the answers you provide? Perhaps you will be brave enough to allow someone to videotape you so you can observe yourself in an interview and eliminate any ticks or tells you may find "annoying."

CHAPTER 12
Negotiating Compensation

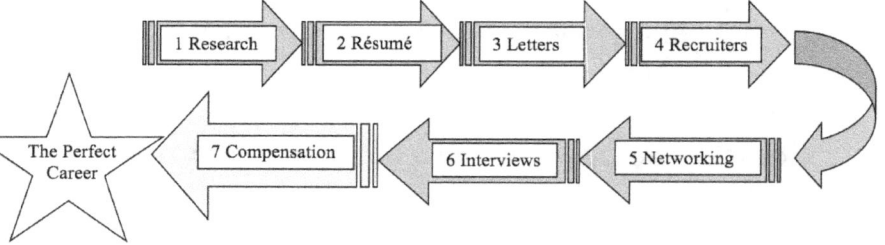

Once the job has been identified, you have sent your résumé in, the interview has been completed and the offer to employ you submitted, you will be given the opportunity to negotiate your compensation package. Often, individuals feel they are at a disadvantage when negotiating their compensation because they need the job, and the organization is in a power position. While this is often the case, it is important to realize that at the point that the offer is submitted to you, the organization has decided that it is YOU they want. Yes, after all the interviews, the other candidates, and the review of perhaps hundreds of résumés, it has boiled down to YOU as the one they see as the best fit for the open position. As we discussed before, finding out why they need to hire someone is a key piece of information for you to gain during the interview process. Apart from being better able to answer their questions during the interview process, now is when this information will be of value to you.

During the interview process, you asked them why they have decided to hire someone in this position. They relay to you that one of their middle-level managers has left to join a competitor, and they need to replace them. BINGO, key information here. It is VERY important that they hire someone quickly. So now you have increased your power of negotiation with this information.

Negotiation is the act of communication in order to have a meeting of the minds. Usually both parties start from different perspectives of needs and must reach an agreement. When you negotiate to purchase your car, the difference is that the dealer wants to get you to pay as much as possible, and you want to end up paying as little as possible. The gap between what you want to pay and what the dealer wants you to pay is that difference. During the negotiation process, you both work to see if there is a way to bridge that gap. It might not be just financial considerations but could be other things such as throwing in a set of car mats or perhaps free first service or some other item of value that you may need.

One cardinal rule during salary negotiations:

"THE FIRST PERSON TO MENTION A NUMBER LOSES."

Why is this so important? Let's take a look at a brief salary negotiation process between a potential employer and a job candidate. In this case, the employer has a maximum budget of $55,000 for the position. James (the candidate) has a goal of $43,000 salary, and a minimum of $39,000:

EMPLOYER: "Well, James, it looks like you are the best candidate, and we would like to offer you the position."

JAMES: "That's great, Mrs. Harris! I am happy to accept, and I'm sure you'll be pleased with my productivity and results."

MRS. HARRIS: "We are very excited about bringing you on board. What are your salary expectations?"

JAMES: "Well, I after conducting research and finding out what comparable positions make, I think that a starting salary of $43,000 would be agreeable."

So, what has just happened here? Basically, James has shortchanged his starting salary by a whopping 21%! He left $12,000 on the table. So how can James avoid losing this much money and increase his salary? The first rule he broke was mentioning a number. Once he did that, the employer knew she did not have to go above that and might even be able to negotiate a little bit lower. Also notice that James did NOT use soft control by asking a question at the end of each response.

Let's take a look at a different outcome with the same scenario of the employer's salary budget and James' salary expectations:

MRS. HARRIS: "Well, James, it looks like you are the best candidate, and we would like to offer you the position."

JAMES: "That's great, Mrs. Harris! I am happy to accept, and I'm sure you'll be pleased with my productivity and results."

MRS. HARRIS: "We are very excited about bringing you on board. What are your salary expectations?"

JAMES: "Well, Mrs. Harris, to be honest, I want to make sure that both you and I are happy with the salary we negotiate. So may I ask what your budget is for this position?"

MRS. HARRIS: "If I'm not mistaken, the salary has been budgeted for $55,000. Is that in your range?"

JAMES: "Would you be open to perhaps a situation in which I work for the first 90 days at $55,000, and if I perform to a satisfactory level, we would be able to increase that to $57,000?"

At this point, Mrs. Harris might state that she has gone to the absolute top of her salary range, but she may have some additional room to work with between her and the HR office. In this case, James deliberately put the question of salary back onto the organization and hiring manager. While James would have been temporarily happy with the initial salary number he had in mind, after a short period of time, he would have started comparing what he was making with others in similar jobs and positions and found out that he was underpaid. However, James was a client of mine and was able to apply the lessons of "whoever mentions a number first loses." He got the organization to mention their number first.

Sometimes you may get an organization or hiring manager who is adamant about getting you to tell them your salary requirements. In this case, we are back to conducting research to find out what a comparable salary would be for a similar position in this and other companies in the specific geographic location that the organization is located. I mention this because the cost of living in various parts of the country can be quite different. As of this writing, a $50,000 salary in Raleigh, North Carolina would need to be $69,418 in Los Angeles, California. That is a difference of almost $20,000. Fairly significant.

There are several places you can find salary comparisons. Just a few are:

CNN Money - http://money.cnn.com/calculator/pf/cost-of-living/

Salary.com - http://www.salary.com/

Indeed.com - http://www.indeed.com/salary

When an organization wants you to divulge what your previous salary was, it is okay to state, "I've done research and found that for someone in my position, with my background, I would be worth a salary of between $50,000-$60,000."

One outstanding book for learning the techniques and strategies of negotiation is Roger Fisher, Bruce Patton, and William Ury's book *Getting to Yes: Negotiating Without Giving In* (2011). In their book, Fisher, Ury, and Patton state that you should develop a realistic minimum salary, or your bottom line. This is the point at which you will not go below and from which you are willing to walk away. Knowing your minimum total compensation is crucial to your negotiating power.

Negotiation, like any communication flow, is a process. The compensation negotiation process uses the following basic framework:

Step 1 – Preparation. In this, probably the MOST important stage of the negotiation process, you will find out what the employer's needs are and why you are the best person for the opening. You will define your bottom line for the negotiations after having conducted salary research for the position, the industry, the organization, and the geographic location. (Note: define your bottom line for yourself, not with the intent of divulging it to the organization.)

Step 2 – Exchanging Information. During this non-confrontational process, both you and the employer try to take a position and make a case for it by putting your favorable information on the table. Obtaining information is crucial at this stage. Questions such as, "What did the previous person make in this job?" and, "What do you have budgeted for the position?" will provide you with a specific range or, better yet, a specific dollar amount that the employer has budgeted for the salary of the position.

Additionally, as noted, the financial aspect of your compensation package is only one portion. We will be discussing all of the various aspects of compensation and how you might work those into the entire package. At the very least, it will be worthwhile to ask about these items. From a philosophical viewpoint, the worst thing they can say is, "No." But if you do not ask, you will never know the answer.

Step 3 – Provide your idea of a fair compensation package. You might typically state this as the full package that you anticipated or just the salary. Salary, as we will see in a few moments, is NOT the only form of compensation, but it is usually the starting point.

Step 4 – Watch the non-verbal behaviors (or if on the phone, how long the silence is) after you mention that figure.

Step 5 – The company will typically come back with a counteroffer.

Step 6 – Evaluate their sincerity and commitment to that counteroffer. If it seems hard-line, then you may want to evaluate if you can accept it. Or if it seems to be flexible, you may want to provide yet another counteroffer or at this stage begin to explore other parts of the compensation package.

On the next page is a short overview of the process:

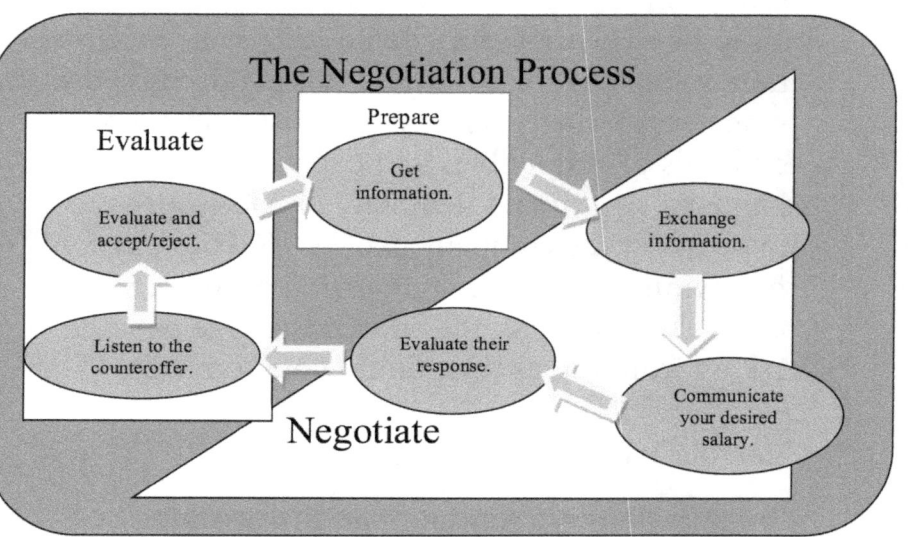

Salary Isn't the ONLY Compensation

Many times, individuals feel that salary is the only, or at least the most important, aspect of the compensation negotiation process. There are so many other aspects to compensation that can be worked with through the hiring manager and the organization's HR department. Some of these items will of course depend on the level of your employment, but many can be worked into the package apart from the salary issue.

The organization sometimes has insurances such as health, vision, dental, and chiropractic care in a buffet-style benefit package. You get to pick some of the benefits but not all of them. You may have a family, so your family dental coverage may be more important than 2 days a year at the company bungalow on the beach. You can also select different levels of deductibles and copays with some of the plans. This could definitely impact your take-home pay if the company expects YOU to pay for the premiums or a specific portion of them. Some organizations pay for the entire insurance package. Ask up front rather than finding out too late.

Flexible Work Time

Organizations are finding that dual working couples are having a difficult time finding childcare. And as our parents get older, many of us need to take care of them, so working a flexible schedule can pay off.

There are various types of flexible work times. Some organizations may have a "core" set of hours you need to be at work. One example is that you have to work 8 hours a day and be at the workplace between 9-2. You can slide either earlier or later. A 6-2 schedule might work for you to avoid traffic, then pick up the kids from school at 3.

Flexible Work Place

Many organizations are finding that employees can

work effectively from places other than at the office. The benefit for the organization is less electricity, less concern over parking, reduced stress for the employees, and more productive employees. Some organizations simply want you to get results. Best Buy, Google, and others call this a ROWE (Results Only Work Environment). In his 2009 landmark book *Drive: The Surprising Truth About What Motivates Us*, Daniel Pink points out that many organizations are finding the value in this type of workplace. Be on the lookout for this as a negotiation point. You may be able to work from home, the coffee shop, a university, or virtually anyplace you can get an Internet connection.

Hardware

Be aware that cell phones, laptops, company automobiles, and other types of incentives can also be included in the compensation package. Clearly, they should be needed as a result of the job type you are doing. If you are a trainer and have to visit several sites each week, having a company car makes sense. Otherwise, you are billing the company for the miles you drive at a designated reimbursement rate. A cell phone is another perk that you might be able to negotiate. Tablets and laptops are also in this same area. However, beware of the electronic leash. If the company gives you tools to be able to work away from the office, they will likely want to contact you away from the office at virtually any time.

Bonuses

While not exactly non-financial, your ability to produce may come with a bonus structure as well. Make sure you ask about it. I had one client who worked for a company for a year before finding out that there was a bonus structure for sales over a certain amount. Imagine his surprise when he found out that he was supposed to be getting a few thousand dollars as a result of his performance.

Stock Options

There are many different stock option packages that are out there. It is beyond the scope of this book to discuss the nuances of the value and leveraging of stock options, but it is a compensation aspect to consider.

Ultimately, you want to be happy in your position. Compensation is very important, but not as important as the job and organization itself. No matter what an organization will pay you, you have to be able to hold your head up and be proud of your contributions as well as knowing that you make a difference in the job, the organization, and the world as a result of what you do.

As previously mentioned, I often ask students in my human resources class, "If I were going to pay you $100,000 a year to do any job, what would you do?" It is amazing how many of them are stumped. What would YOU do for $100,000 a year? Is it the same thing you would do for $10,000 a year? If you are in the right career, it is. When it is the right career, you will know it.

Chapter 12 Summary

- When it comes down to negotiating salary and compensation between you and the organization, ***the first person to mention a number loses.***
- Negotiation is a two-way process.
- Salary isn't the only compensation.

Chapter 12 Action Plan

Today: Write down what your dream job would provide you with as minimum compensation.

Tomorrow: Investigate the web for jobs you want and what they offer.

This week: Practice negotiating for a hypothetical job with a friend or colleague playing the role of the interviewer. Then switch roles and ask someone else to play the candidate while YOU are the interviewer.

Chapter 13

Your First 90 Days – Do I Still Have to Work Here?

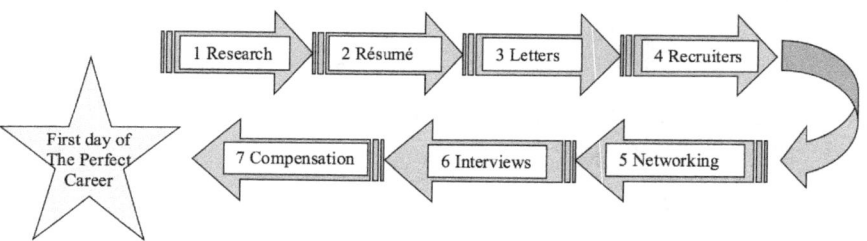

Throughout the course of this book, we have discussed many of the different aspects of the job search. We have reviewed the importance of aligning the components of your Career Search System, research, résumé, cover letters, interviews, and compensation with your desired career direction. We have looked at the specifics of a quality résumé, impactful letters, and energetic and realistic interview responses. These are merely the tools to GET you to the career. Now what? How will you KNOW if this is the career for you? Many individuals end up suffering because they simply do not know any better. They COULD explore new careers.

After being hired, a new employee is not expected to be highly productive immediately, regardless of what they say in the interview: "The candidate must hit the ground running!" or, "We expect employees to contribute to the bottom line immediately!" Organizations realize that new employees take some time to get acclimated, find their way around, and eventually contribute to the organization.

Figure 13-1 – Productivity-Acclimation chart

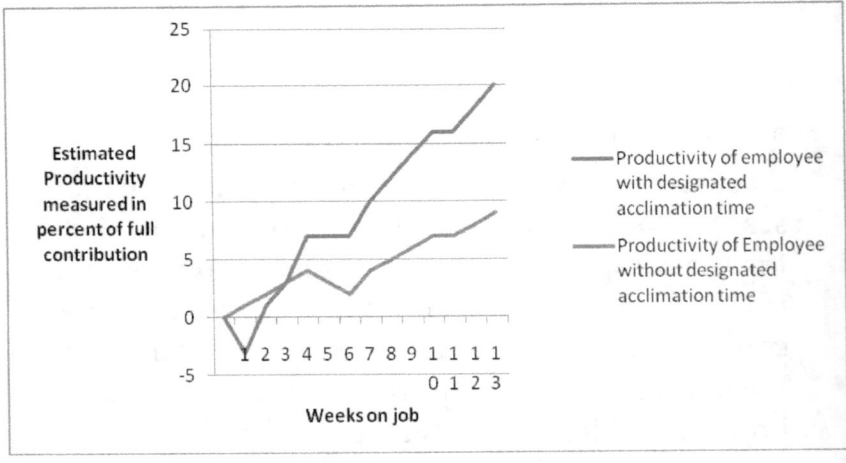

The process of helping to move a new employee to full capability through the "onboarding" process is a lengthy one. Many organizations have a formal orientation training or set of classes that new hires must attend, at which the CEO or other leader addresses the team to let them know they are important to the future of the company. Others simply allow employees to get used to the company by "getting to work."

Your primary concern during that first 90 days and during the "onboarding" process is to continually evaluate the fit between the organization's cultural values and yours. If the fit is not there, you will still have the career search momentum, ready to find a new position. It is entirely possible that another position is available within the organization that might be a better fit. Once you have become familiar with the structure and processes within the organization, you will be in a better position to evaluate the entire organization.

Find a Mentor

One of the best ways that has been shown time and time again to be effective is to assign a mentor to new employees. Not just anyone, but someone who has a proven track record of performance and understands how the organization works. A mentor is someone who may be influential in the organization. A mentoring relationship is a relationship that is developmental in which the mentor shares information and skills gleaned through experience with their protégé.

Mentoring is a powerful tool that is a developmental partnership. Picking the right individual to be your mentor can mean the difference between a successfully developed "mentor-protégé" experience and one that simply does not meet its potential. The role of mentorship in the career development of employees CAN be a wonderful experience. We can think of it as the pinnacle of employee guidance.

The below illustration shows the various levels of employee guidance. While it is certainly not necessary to progress through each of these levels to find a mentor, it helps to understand who conducts the levels within your new organization.

Figure 13-2 – Taxonomy of Employee Guidance.

The selection of highly effective mentors is of utmost importance to the rapid and smooth transition from a "new employee" to a trusted member of the organization. Organizations with an effective mentoring program experience many benefits. The transfer of informal but important knowledge, also called "tribal" knowledge, is crucial. Whom do you see when you need something specific? What are the support mechanisms in place? And what does it REALLY take to get ahead in this organization? The mentor must have a good sense of self and know when they are needed and when they should actually task the new employee with finding information on their own. It is a slippery slope when a mentor gets TOO involved in the assimilation of a new employee. You do not want them to become a babysitter, just a resource. More often than not, a new employee must rely on their supervisor for this mentoring support. Several problems arise with this scenario.

Supervisors will likely also be the key person, if not the only person, conducting the performance evaluation on their employees. A new employee wants to provide a very good first impression, so he will probably not go to the supervisor with a problem lest they look like they cannot take care of themselves.

Supervisors are also responsible for many employees, and spending too much time with one employee can look like favoritism. A mentor or sponsor can take this task away from the supervisor, freeing this time so they can focus on more pressing issues.

Find a mentor who can help you understand the culture of the organization. A good one will typically tell you that, while you are doing a good job, there are even better ways of getting things done. A good mentor will not let YOU be satisfied with the quality of your work but will encourage you to do more to find out how the quality can continue to improve. Eventually, you will find someone knocking on YOUR door asking questions of you. Guess what? YOU'RE A MENTOR!!!

Acceptance Stage

Most career search and job search books end when you accept your offer for employment and begin working for a company. In truth, the job search has not ended; it is merely entering the acceptance stage for you and the organization. You simply cannot know whether you will fit into the culture of the organization, or not until you experience the people, policies, procedures, and protocols that all organizations have in place. The person-organization fit is one of extreme importance to you in your continuing search. Many industries have companies with similar missions and products but in which the actual cultures of the organizations are vastly different. In one, there may be very rigid structure—so much so that if you step outside your office and walk down the hall, you are not expected to greet or acknowledge other people as it may be seen as interfering with their work. In another organization, your primary job is merely a placeholder for your interaction with the many other employees in the organization. You may be expected to not only do your primary job but also have many collateral positions such as additional search committees, policy committees, advisory boards, and other jobs.

The amount of flexibility of your job may well be determined by your immediate supervisor, the actual structure of the organization, and, in some cases, by a very strict manual outlining all acceptable and unacceptable behaviors. In the case of a very rigid organization, you may not have any flexibility for overtime, personal time, or other jobs. Yet, in another organization, they may want you to rely on your own judgment for all aspects of your position.

One company in England, W. L. Gore, has a very flexible structure as it contributes significantly to the productivity and innovation on which they built the organization. You may know one of the products as "GoreTex." They have innovated many different products over the years. Their main one was a fabric that was breathable but kept water only to one side. This fabric brought forth many applications including shoes, tents, sleeping bags, and backpacks. The organization prides itself on the environment and flexibility that it provides employees to be creative. Individuals are not assigned to a specific team but rather are free to work on products in which they have interest. An individual seeking work in this area must have a personality that will match this type of organization. An individual with a very "realistic" personality type that needs structure to feel comfortable would clearly not function very well here.

Immediately after getting hired, it is not unusual to be asked how you like your new position and to respond with an unequivocal and enthusiastic, "I love it here!" This is likely true due to the relief from finding employment, finding out that you do have skills that are needed, and the excitement of finding out about new opportunities. Additionally, we as humans are unlikely to rapidly admit to a mistake that quickly after we make it.

It is similar to purchasing a new car. Imagine if a friend asked, "Nice Cadillac. How do you like it?" You do not often hear a response like, "I really hate it. I spent $55,000 on it, but it's not nearly what I want." We would rather convince ourselves that we did not make the mistake. The truth is, even if we question our decision to join an organization that is not aligned with our career goals, we will tolerate it for a period of time before we are convinced that we did, indeed, make a career mistake. And it happens more often than people really like to admit.

Once you are hired and have been with the company for about 30 days, you will have met your new coworkers, found out where the various support mechanisms are, and learned a little bit about the leadership in the organization. Several years ago, one of my clients, a hard-working instructional designer, was hired by a large Fortune 500 bank. She was thrilled about working for a company that had more than 30,000 employees and was looking to strategically grow significantly over the next 5 years. Her immediate supervisor had been with the company 2 years. Her initial assignment was to develop training materials, web-based and hard copy, to support the recently completed management training and development strategy.

The strategy was straightforward; the client knew her trade, but the methods of design and delivery were very rigid and structured, so much so that the instructional designer felt very stifled in her position. After several discussions with the human resources office, the manager, and several layers above, it was decided that the fit of the individual and the organization simply was not a good one. Both agreed that it was in the best interest of the individual and the organization to sever the relationship.

Several months went by, and the immediate supervisor who had previously been there was transferred to another division. The new supervisor contacted the instructional designer and rehired her back, not as an employee, but as a consultant. In this case, the creativity to develop the training platforms for the organization was in place, the designer crafted some wonderfully innovative and effective training classes and tools, and the actual model was not only used for the specific branch but accepted and implemented company-wide as a training methodology that worked for that company.

One organization that has found out that an early person-organization fit discovery is worthwhile is Netflix. The organization found that it is simply not worthwhile to retain employees who do not fit within the organization. In fact, Netflix would rather pay a poorly performing employee to leave than to pay them for mediocre or worse performance. You can view the Netflix values statement online at http://www.slideshare.net/reed2001/culture-1798664.

The first 90 days on the job is your opportunity to explore the organization and the culture. Find out who and where the informal power structure is. Discuss with your supervisor what the performance appraisal system looks like, and find out what behaviors/responsibilities outside of the primary job's are expected. The following is a short list of questions that you should explore during the first 90 days to determine the level of fit you have with the organization:

- What are the performance standards I must meet?

- What are the rules (written and unspoken) for personal time?

- Are there clubs, organizations, or other support mechanisms for special groups such as ethnically focused, veterans based, or special interests?

- What are the expectations for additional tasks that might exist outside the formal job description?

- Obtain a copy of any performance appraisal forms that will be used to evaluate your performance. If it is an electronic system, ask HR for a quick overview to get a feel for the performance criteria you will be evaluated against.

A system is no better than the quality of the components that go into it. You must continue to improve the quality of the components of your

Career Search System. If your résumé is not getting you the interviews you desire, it may be time to revise the keywords, accomplishments, or wording of your responsibility set. If the interviews seem to be falling flat, ask a friend to evaluate your responses. If your negotiation techniques result in organizations telling you they cannot afford you, you may have too high of a salary expectation. The components of the system should be finely-tuned up during you career search. An old saying holds that "Insanity is doing the same thing over and over again expecting different results." Keep your career search system tuned through continued research, exploration, networking, and education.

Conclusion

The beginning of your new career is a crucial time. Typically the first 90 days in a new organization are among the most stressful you will experience. There are bound to be some very high points while at the same time you will experience some frustrations as you learn new ways of doing business as well as identifying the key people within the organization.

The key to a successful first 90 days is to make sure you communicate. Ask a lot of questions; it is expected. Explore individuals outside of your immediate area, and ask how they fit into the organization. Let them know you are new, what your job is, and what you hope you can contribute to the organization. You are learning a new culture and new set of processes, procedures, and policies. This is the time when you should realize this and enjoy the product of your Career Search System. Be friendly, be observant, and be sensitive to the new culture. After all, you will be adjusting to a new culture, and it probably will not change to meet your needs.

Chapter 13 Summary

- Your first 90 days is both the most stressful and likely the most energetic you'll feel at an organization.

- Ask questions that provide you with a feel for the company and its culture.

- Meet new people outside your immediate area and explore how their roles/functions fit into the organization.

- Understand how the organization defines "performance."

- Ask for feedback on the quality of your product or performance often.

COVER LETTER EXAMPLES

Informational Interview Request/No Résumé

Homer Sympsan   1234 Deadwood Ave.
                                                                                                                       San Diego, CA 92131

Date

Decision Maker, Title
Company Name
Address
City, State Zip

Dear Name of Decision Maker:

Recently, I decided that I would like to explore new careers and industries. That is my purpose in writing to you. Perhaps you might be willing to meet for 10 to 15 minutes for that purpose. I am confident that our shared backgrounds in XXXXX will provide a mutually interesting and informative meeting.

In one of my recent positions, I was a product manager of a global paint company. Upon my assignment, I conducted a rapid initial survey to determine the status of the product. Reviewing critical aspects of success for product sales, I identified new markets in developing countries. In two of these countries, sales had actually declined. Completely replacing the marketing materials with new multimedia materials, I found that the sales teams were not familiar enough with the sales tools or the product itself. I instituted a one-week seminar for all regional sales representatives for the product. Sales for the first year increased by $5M with a corresponding increase in profits of $1.03M.

Because I am aware that many opportunities arise before they become "advertised", I realize that getting to know fellow professionals such as yourself should be an important part of my strategy. The opportunity to exchange ideas and develop contacts with other XXXXXXX professionals would be deeply appreciated.

I realize most senior-level positions are filled through recruiting or networking and rarely advertised. I am aware of the importance of getting to know fellow professionals such as you. The opportunity to exchange ideas and develop contacts with other professionals would be deeply appreciated and is all I am seeking.

I will call your office in a few days to introduce myself and to set a brief meeting. I want to thank you in advance for any assistance and advice you might be able to provide.

Sincerely,

Homer Sympsan
555-121-2121

Information Meeting/Venture Capitalists / No Résumé

Homer Sympsan   1234 Deadwood Ave.
                                                                                                                                      San Diego, CA 92131

Date

Decision Maker, Title
Company Name
Address
City, State Zip

Dear Name of Decision Maker:

[I am looking for an opportunity to apply my management leadership in directing divestitures, acquisitions and rapid growth to a new environment. Perhaps within your portfolio of clients, there may be a need for someone with my skills and expertise.] OR [I am looking for an opportunity to apply my leadership in directing strategic alliances, new product introductions and international marketing to a new environment. As you become aware of opportunities in the XXXXX marketplace, perhaps you might have a need for my skills and expertise in one of your business ventures.]

In one of my recent positions, I was the President of Springfield Paints. Upon my assignment, I conducted a rapid initial survey to determine the status of the organization. Reviewing critical aspects of success for the organization, I identified sales and overall profits as unremarkable over several prior years. Sales had actually declined. Completely replacing the senior management staff of VP Operations, VP Sales/Marketing, controller, and key salesman, I instituted a companywide cost reduction program. Sales for the first year increased by $55M with a corresponding increase in profits of $10.3M.

As a venture capitalist, your ear is "close to the ground" regarding new business opportunities here in the XXXXX area. With that in mind, I am requesting a brief meeting where we could exchange industry knowledge, and possibly you may be aware of others who might be willing to meet with me for networking purposes or who might have a need for my skills.

I will contact you in a few days to determine a time when we might meet. I look forward to talking to you. Thank you in advance.

Sincerely,

Homer Sympsan
555-121-2121

Alumni Letter/No Resume Enclosed

Homer Sympsan   1234 Deadwood Ave.
                                                                                                 San Diego, CA 92131

Date

Decision Maker, Title
Company Name
Address
City, State Zip

Dear Name of Decision Maker:

As a fellow Alumni of XXXXX, I have need of your knowledge and insights on the XXXXX job market. This is a favor I would gladly reciprocate in the future.

While I realize how busy we all are these days, I was hoping you might be willing to extend a few minutes of your time to network and exchange ideas. The purpose of this requested meeting would be simply to network. I hope to take advantage of my prestigious alumni community to explore the XXXXX job market. Getting to know professionals such as yourself will be an enjoyable part my career search. I would welcome the opportunity to exchange ideas with you.

I will call you in a few days to introduce myself and to determine a time when we might meet. Thank you in advance for any assistance and advice you might be able to provide.

Sincerely,

Homer Sympsan
555-121-2121

Advice or Influentials Based on a Referral/No Résumé

Homer Sympsan   1234 Deadwood Ave.
                           San Diego, CA 92131

Date

Decision Maker, Title
Company Name
Address
City, State Zip

Dear Name of Decision Maker:

Having spoken to _____ regarding career opportunities within the XXXXX area, he/she suggested contacting you. While I am looking for a new position, the purpose of this letter is not to seek employment from you but rather to request a brief meeting to network and exchange ideas.

Recently, I chose to leave a senior-level management position within the XXXXX field to seek a new position. As I seek to determine a new direction for my future, I plan to contact a few professionals within the XXXXX community to get their insights. Perhaps you might be willing to meet for 10 to 15 minutes for that purpose. I am confident that our shared backgrounds in the XXXXXX industry will provide a mutually interesting and informative meeting.

In one of my recent positions, I was the President of Springfield Paints. Upon my assignment, I conducted a rapid initial survey to determine the status of the organization. Reviewing critical aspects of success for the organization, I identified sales and overall profits as unremarkable over several prior years. Sales had actually declined. Completely replacing the senior management staff of VP Operations, VP Sales/Marketing, controller, and key salesman, I instituted a company-wide cost reduction program. Sales for the first year increased by $55M with a corresponding increase in profits of $10.3M.

Because I am aware that many opportunities arise before they become "advertised," I realize that getting to know fellow professionals such as you should be an important part of my strategy. The opportunity to exchange ideas and develop contacts with other XXXXXX professionals would be deeply appreciated.

I will be calling you within the next few days to introduce myself and to set a brief meeting. I want to thank you in advance for any assistance and advice you might be able to provide. I look forward to meeting you.

Sincerely,

Homer Sympsan
555-121-2121

The 21st Century Career Search System

Direct Employer/Targeted/No Résumé Included

Homer Sympsan　　　　　　　　　　　　　　　　　　　1234 Deadwood Ave.
　　　　　　　　　　　　　　　　　　　　　　　　　　　　San Diego, CA 92131

Date

Decision Maker, Title
Company Name
Address
City, State Zip

Dear Name of Decision Maker:

If you are looking for an addition to your senior management team, my letter will be of great interest to you. As a senior XXXXXX manager with more than 20 years management experience within the XXXXX area, I would like to be considered for openings on your senior management team.

In one of my recent positions, I was the President of Springfield Paints. Upon my assignment, I conducted a rapid initial survey to determine the status of the organization. Reviewing critical aspects of success for the organization, I identified sales and overall profits as unremarkable over several prior years. Sales had actually declined. Completely replacing the senior management staff of VP Operations, VP Sales/Marketing, controller, and key salesman, I instituted a company-wide cost reduction program. Sales for the first year increased by $55M with a corresponding increase in profits of $10.3M.

I would be interested in talking to you further to discuss how my background could contribute to your organization's growth and profitability. I will call your office in a few days to arrange a convenient time to meet. I look forward to meeting with you.

Sincerely,

Homer Sympsan
555-121-2121

Events—Can be Used as a Direct Approach Letter/Résumé or for Spot Opportunities

Homer Sympsan   1234 Deadwood Ave.
                                                                                             San Diego, CA 92131

Date

Decision Maker, Title
Company Name
Address
City, State Zip

Dear Name of Decision Maker:

Recently, the *(insert newspaper or whatever source)* contained an interesting article about *(name of company)*, which dealt with the probability of your expanding your *(insert related skill or product)*. *(Discuss the parts of the article that you feel particularly well suited to address.)* As I read this article, I found myself particularly interested in your company and in being part of your new expansion. That is why I am writing directly to you.

In one of my recent positions, I was the President of Springfield Paints. Upon my assignment, I conducted a rapid initial survey to determine the status of the organization. Reviewing critical aspects of success for the organization, I identified sales and overall profits as unremarkable over several prior years. Sales had actually declined. Completely replacing the senior management staff of VP Operations, VP Sales/Marketing, controller, and key salesman, I instituted a company-wide cost reduction program. Sales for the first year increased by $55M with a corresponding increase in profits of $10.3M.

The opportunity to discuss your plans would provide insight into a possible association. I will call your office early next week to arrange an appointment. I look forward to talking with you.

Sincerely,

Homer Sympsan
555-121-2121

Enclosure
Letter #5/Ads - Blind or Identified/w or w/o Résumé

Homer Sympsan　　　　　　　　　　　　　　　　　　　1234 Deadwood Ave.
　　　　　　　　　　　　　　　　　　　　　　　　　　　　San Diego, CA 92131

Date

Decision Maker, Title
Company Name
Address
City, State Zip

Dear Name of Decision Maker:

Please accept this letter as application for the _____ position currently available with your company as advertised in the _____.

In one of my recent positions, I was the President of Springfield Paints. Upon my assignment, I conducted a rapid initial survey to determine the status of the organization. Reviewing critical aspects of success for the organization, I identified sales and overall profits as unremarkable over several prior years. Sales had actually declined. Completely replacing the senior management staff of VP Operations, VP Sales/Marketing, controller, and key salesman, I instituted a company-wide cost reduction program. Sales for the first year increased by $55M with a corresponding increase in profits of $10.3M.

Your Requirements	My Qualifications
1.	1.
2.	2.
3.	3.
etc.	

I look forward to hearing from you in the near future to schedule a personal meeting, during which I hope to learn more about the position, your company's plans and goals, and to explore how I can contribute to the success of your organization.

Sincerely,

Homer Sympsan
555-121-2121

In the event that the organization wants you to provide an exact salary, one of my suggested phrases is: "I will submit a salary history and other personal information at such time as you indicate serious interest in my qualifications." (OR ... respond with a range that includes an entire compensation package, i.e., benefits, retirement, etc.)

Enclosure
Colleagues, Friends and Acquaintances/ Résumé Enclosed

Homer Sympsan　　　　　　　　　　　　　　　　　　　　1234 Deadwood Ave.
　　　　　　　　　　　　　　　　　　　　　　　　　　　　　San Diego, CA 92131

Date

Decision Maker, Title
Company Name
Address
City, State Zip

Dear Name of Decision Maker:

While you don't often receive letters from me, I have an important reason for writing now. **XX Insert personalized info here XX** I wanted to let you know of this change in my situation and ask for your advice and input. Part of my career search strategy is contacting a few friends who might be kind enough to "keep their eyes open" and share thoughts and ideas as to industries I should contact.

I was hoping that you might take a moment to review the enclosed résumé. As you can see, I would like to find a position as a **XXXXXX**. I would certainly enjoy another position **XXXXXX** but would be open to exploring new industries as well. I am confident my strengths are applicable within a broad range of industries. Your suggestions and ideas as to industries to contact would be very encouraging. I am open to any avenues you suggest.

Additionally, I am interested in expanding my circle of acquaintances. It seems that you may, possibly, be able to provide me with a few select introductions. Any names of individuals who might be of help to me or who can direct me to others would be greatly appreciated. The more contacts I make, the more opportunities I can uncover.

If you have any thoughts or ideas, please jot them down. I will contact you in a week or so to discuss your ideas. Thank you in advance for your help.

Sincerely,

Homer Sympsan
555-121-2121

Enclosure
Search Firms & Employment Agencies/ Résumé Enclosed

Homer Sympsan	1234 Deadwood Ave. San Diego, CA 92131

Date

Decision Maker, Title
Company Name
Address
City, State Zip

Dear Name of Decision Maker:

I understand that your firm has an excellent record of matching senior XXXXX executives with top organizations. After reviewing my credentials, I am sure you will agree that I would be a serious candidate for a senior XXXXX position for one of your clients. While I have included a resume for your perusal, the following bullets briefly highlight my successes:

In one of my recent positions, I was the President of Springfield Paints. Upon my assignment, I conducted a rapid initial survey to determine the status of the organization. Reviewing critical aspects of success for the organization, I identified sales and overall profits as unremarkable over several prior years. Sales had actually declined. Completely replacing the senior management staff of VP Operations, VP Sales/Marketing, controller, and key salesman, I instituted a company-wide cost reduction program. Sales for the first year increased by $55M with a corresponding increase in profits of $10.3M.

My demonstrated skills at managing hi-tech teams to expand business opportunities would be most valued by a leading XXXXXXXX organization desiring a competitive advantage. Relocation would not be an issue. I look forward to hearing from you.

Sincerely,

Homer Sympsan
555-121-2121

Letter to References/Enclosed Résumé/ Enclosed List of References

(You'll want to put the list of references on a separate page to serve as an attachment. Be sure to include names, addresses, email addresses and telephone numbers. Use only those references who you have control over.)

Homer Sympsan 1234 Deadwood Ave.
San Diego, CA 92131

Date

Decision Maker, Title
Company Name
Address
City, State Zip

Dear Name of Decision Maker:

Thank you for your willingness to serve as a reference during my career search.

As my campaign gains momentum, you will undoubtedly receive calls from potential employers with whom I have been in contact. I felt it would be helpful for you to have some information available that would highlight my work experience and qualifications. You are probably familiar with most of my background, but I have attached a current résumé so you can review it. Hopefully, it will assist you in answering any details.

I am also enclosing a list of others who have agreed to be references for me. Many potential employers will ask for additional names of individuals whom they may contact. I have sent each one of my references the same information I am enclosing for you. You may wish to consider one or more of these names when you are requested to provide additional references.

Thank you again for your support during my search campaign. I would appreciate your contacting me when there is activity from a potential employer.

In any event, I will be contacting you periodically to keep you advised of my progress.

Sincerely,

Homer Sympsan
555-121-2121

Follow-up Interview/To be Mailed Within 24 Hours After Your Interview

Homer Sympsan	1234 Deadwood Ave. San Diego, CA 92131

Date

Decision Maker, Title
Company Name
Address
City, State Zip

Dear Name of Decision Maker:

The position we discussed *Friday* offers considerable opportunity and challenge. After rethinking our discussion, I am convinced that I can make an immediate contribution toward the growth and profitability of *Company Name*.

The following accomplishments are related to our discussion and lend support to my ability to confidently meet any challenges related to this position:

       1.
       2.   CARs, CARs, CARs!!!
       3.

(Select CARs that support the key areas of need that emerged during the interview.)

I am convinced that my proven track record of increasing revenues in each of my past environments, coupled with my skill at creating positive change, can provide both the immediate and long-term results you desire.

I am sincerely interested in an association with *Company Name*. Our discussion was both insightful and productive. Your environment provides the challenges I am seeking and in which I have always been successful. I look forward to speaking with you again on _____.

Sincerely,

Homer Sympsan
555-121-2121

Interviewing Questions and Sample Responses

Sample Opening Question

"So tell me a little bit about yourself." – Create a 1-minute "commercial" of yourself. Remember to describe your background and how you will fit the job. Remember to use "Soft Control." Close your response with a question for the interviewer such as, "Do you have similar requirements in your organization?" Do not volunteer personal information (e.g. marital status or number of children.) This is not required of you and is not legal to ask in the interview process.

Sample Response

"I am an expert marketer with more than 5 years of experience in global marketing of heavy equipment repair parts. In my most recent job, I was responsible for delivery of replacement parts for construction equipment at a remote location in the Saudi desert. I was able to develop a system that leveraged the nearest airport, a private one, and resulted in an average delivery time of less than 48 hours, effectively saving the contract. Do you have challenges like this in your organization?"

Sample Closed-end Question

"Do you have any special restrictions to your hiring date?"

Sample Response

"No. When would you anticipate a hiring decision to be made?"

Sample Situational Question

"Imagine that it's Friday afternoon, and your supervisor has come down and asked you to keep your team late to get a special project done. How would you deliver this news to your team?"

Sample Response

"I would make it clear to my team that it is important that we complete this special project as it has a direct impact on the success of our organization. They are counting on us, and I am counting on my team. Do you anticipate this problem might come up often?"

About the Author

Bruce Gillies, Psy.D. is a career counselor and faculty member at California Lutheran University where he teaches graduate level and undergraduate level courses in organizational sciences. He holds a doctorate in Industrial/Organizational Psychology. He developed the first online Career Counseling course in California to help individuals seeking LPCC licensure meet the state licensing requirements. While serving in the U. S. Navy for 22 years, he was a career counselor, was the Navy's Senior Transition program specialist, and has written numerous articles about careers, career search, and organizational career development programs. This book is based on over a quarter century of experience as a professor, hiring manager, résumé reviewer, interviewer, leadership coach, career counselor, and career search professional. Dr. Gillies has been presenting seminars, workshops, and writing articles on career search and career development since 1988.

Other Career Search Tools

Career Planning Books

100 Careers in Film and Television:
ISBN 0-7641-2164-2

100 Great Jobs and How to Get Them:
ISBN 1-57023-116-8

100 Jobs in Technology: ISBN 0-02-861431-3

150 Jobs You Can Start Today: ISBN 0-7679-1609-3

200 Best Jobs for College Graduates:
ISBN 1-56370-855-8

Alternatives to the Peace Corps:
ISBN 0-935028-83-8

Alternative Legal Careers: Wetfeet.com

Arco: 100 Best Careers in Crime Fighting:
ISBN 978-0028613970

Arco: 100 Best Careers for Writers and Artists:
ISBN 0-02-861926-9

Be Bold, Create a Career with Impact:
ISBN 0-9790116-0-4

Best Entry Level Jobs, 2007 Edition:
ISBN 0-375-76560-3

Best Entry-Level Jobs: ISBN 0-375-76472-0

Best Jobs for the 21st Century: ISBN 1-59357-240-9

Career Exploration on the Internet:
ISBN 978-0894342400

Career Opportunities in Art: ISBN 0-8160-4246-2

Career Opportunities in Biotechnology and Drug Development: ISBN 978-0879698805

Career Opportunities in Education:
ISBN 0-8160-4224-1

Career Opportunities in International Trade: Chamber of Commerce (213)-580-7581

Career Opportunities in Religion:
ISBN 0-8015-3200-0

Career Opportunities in the Internet, Video Games, and Multimedia: ISBN 978-0-8160-6317-7

Career Opportunities in the Travel Industry:
ISBN 0-8160-4865-7

Career Warfare: ISBN 0-07-141758-3

Careers in Business: ISBN 0-8442-4506-2

Careers in Communication: ISBN 0-8442-6318-4

Careers in Criminology: ISBN 0-7373-0272-0

Careers in Education: ISBN 0-8442-4512-7

Careers in Entertainment: Wetfeet.com

Careers in Engineering: ISBN 0-07-139041-3

Careers in Finance: ISBN 0-8442-2070-1

Careers in the Game Industry: ISBN 0-7357-1307-3

Careers in Management Consulting: ISBN 1-57851-191-7

Careers for Good Samaritans and Other Humanitarian Types: ISBN 0-07-145879-4

Changing Careers: ISBN 0-534-20766-9

College Handbook: ISBN 0-87447-506-6

Compensation Management in a Knowledge-Based World: ISBN 0-13-086682-2

Complete Guide to Environmental Careers in the 21st Century: ISBN 1-55963-585-1

Cool Careers for Dummies, 3rd Edition: ISBN 978-0-470-11774-3

Creating a Life Worth Living: ISBN 0-06-095243-1

Cyberspace Job Search Kit: ISBN 1-56370-671-7

Directory of Business Information Resources: Pamphlet #0-939300-26-5

Directory of Environmental Websites:
ISSN 1096-3316

Directory of Volunteer Opportunities: Catholic Network (202) 332-1611

Earth Work: ISBN 0-06-258531-2

Employment Outlook, 1996-2006: BLS Projections

Enhanced Occupational Outlook Handbook:
ISBN 1-56370-523-0

Event Planning Careers:
ISBN 0-07-138228-3

Everything You Need to Know about College Sports Recruiting: ISBN 0-8362-2184-2

FBI Careers: ISBN 1-56370-890-6

Forensic Science Careers: ISBN 0-658-00102-7

From Graduation to Corporation:
ISBN 978-1-4389-3063-3

Get Into Law School: Strategic Approach -
ISBN 0-7432-4103-7

Getting a Raise in 7 days: ISBN 1-57023-099-4

Going to Law School: ISBN 0-471-14907-1

Good Green Jobs: ISBN 0-9605750-6-5

Graduates' Guide to Business Success:
ISBN 1-888069-06-6

Graduate Schools in the U.S.: ISBN 0-7689-1185-0

Great Jobs for History Majors: ISBN 0-658-01061-1

Great Jobs for Math Majors: ISBN 0-8442-6422-9

Great Jobs for Political Science Majors: ISBN 0-8442-4724-3

Great Jobs for Psychology Majors: ISBN 0-658-00452-2

Green at Work: ISBN 1-55963-334-4

Guide to America's Federal Jobs: ISBN 1-56370-526-5

Guide to College Majors: ISBN 0-375-76276-0

Guide to Landing a Career in Law Enforcement: ISBN 0-07-141717-6

Guide to Your Career: ISBN 0-375-76561-1

Health-Care Careers: For the 21st Century ISBN 1-56370-667-9

Hong Kong Employment Guide

How to Get a Job in Southern California: ISBN 0-940625-30-X

How to Get a Job in Europe: ISBN 1-57284-027-7

How to Get the Teaching Job you Want: ISBN 1-57922-029-0

How to Market Yourself: ISBN 0-941817-05-9

I Wanna Be a Sales Rep!: The Insider's Guide to Landing Great-Paying Jobs in Sales
ISBN 978-0966291100

Innovating for Health: ISBN 0-89434-152-9

Insider Guide to Jobs in the Computer Software Industry: Wetfeet.com

Investment Banking: ISBN 1-58131-133-8

International Jobs: Where they are and how to get them - ISBN 978-0738207469

Job Analysis for Chiropractors

Job Hunting for Dummies: ISBN 1-56884-388-7

Job Opportunities for Business Majors:
ISBN 0-7689-0026-3

Job Opportunities for Engineering and Computer Science: ISBN 0-7689-0027-1

Job Opportunities for Health & Science Majors:
ISBN 0-7689-0025-5

Job Searching Online for Dummies:
ISBN 0-7645-0376-6

Jobs for English Majors and Other Smart People:
ISBN 0-87866-391-6

Jobs Rated Almanac: ISBN 0-312-26096-2

JobSmarts 50 Top Careers: ISBN 0-06-095220-2

The Directory of Executive Recruiters:
ISBN 1-885922-77-9

Land your First Job in Film Production:
ISBN 0-943728-91-6

Liberal Arts Power! How to Sell it on Your Résumé:
ISBN 0-87866-254-5

Marketing & Brand Management:
ISBN 1-58131-132-X

Negotiating Salary and Perks: Wetfeet.com

Neuroscience Training Programs in N. America - ANDP (202) 328-9713

New Accountant Careers: ISBN 0-9623351-1-8

New Guide for Occupational Exploration:
ISBN 1-59357-179-8

Newsweek: Careers Yearly - local bookstore

Now, Discover Your Strengths: ISBN 0-7432-0114-0

Opportunities in Event Planning Careers:
ISBN 0-07-138228-3

Opportunities in Marketing Careers:
ISBN 0-8442-1853-7

Opportunities at Home and Abroad Jobs for Travel Lovers: ISBN 10: 1-57023-252-0

Opportunities in Psychology Careers: ISBN 978-0071545303

Job Opportunities for Business and Liberal Arts Graduates: ISBN 1-56079-074-1

Peterson's: Liberal Arts Jobs, 3rd Edition ISBN 0-7689-0148-0

Quick Guide to College Majors and Careers: ISBN 1-56370-834-5

Peterson's: Liberal Arts Jobs - ISBN 0-87866-443-2

Schmoozing: ISBN 1-58131-117-6

Sports Scholarships: ISBN 1-56079-483-6

Starting Your Own Business: ISBN 1-58131-180-X

The Everything Guide to Government Jobs: ISBN 1-59869-078-7

The Everything Alternative Careers Book: ISBN 1-59337-038-5

The Everything Hot Careers Book: ISBN 1-58062-486-3

The Experienced Hand: ISBN 0-910328-33-X

Top Ten Dumb Career Mistakes: ISBN 0-8442-6313-3

The Official Guide to Legal Specialties: ISBN 0-15-900391-1

Today's Hot Job Targets: ISBN 978-1-59357-424-6

The Student's Federal Career Guide: ISBN 0-9647025-6-8

Transitioning to the Nonprofit Sector: ISBN 1-4195-9341-2

Vault Career Guide to Biotech: ISBN 1-58131-268-7

Venture Capital: ISBN 1-58131-131-1

What Color is Your Parachute?: ISBN 1-58008-794-9

What's Your Excuse? Making The Most Of What You Have: ISBN 0-7852-6637-2

Career Opportunities Series (Separate Books):

Advertising and Public Relations, Art, Health Care, Armed Forces, Aviation and Aerospace Industry, Automotive, Banking, Casinos and Casino Hotels, Computers and Cyberspace, Education and Related Services, The Fashion Industry, Film Industry, Finance and Insurance, Health Care, Law Enforcement, Security and Protective Services, Law and the Legal Industry, Library and Information Science, Music Industry, The Nonprofit Sector, Politics, Government and Activism,

Publishing, Science, Sports Industry, Theatre and The Performing Arts, Travel Industry, Radio, and Writing.

REFERENCES

Berra, Y. and Kaplan, D. (2002). *When you come to a Fork in the Road, Take It!: Inspiration and Wisdom from one of Baseball's Greatest Heroes.* Hyperion, New York

Bolles, R. (2013). *What Color is Your Parachute?* Ten Speed Press, New York

Ciardi, M.(Producer), & O'Connor, G.(Director). (2004) *Miracle* [Motion picture]. USA: Pop Pop Productions.

Collins, J. (2001). *Good to Great.* HarperCollins Publishers, New York

Fisher, R., Ury, W., and Patton, B. (2011). *Getting to Yes: Negotiating Agreement Without Giving In,* Penguin, NY

Holland, J. (1959). *A theory of vocational choice.* Journal of Counseling Psychology, Vol 6(1), 1959,

Holland, John. L. (1997). *Making Vocational Choices: A Theory of Vocational Personalities and Work Environments.* Psychological Assessment Resources Inc

Jung, C. (1971). *The Collected Works of C. G. Jung,*

Vol 6: Psychological Types, Princeton University Press, Princeton, NJ

Pink, D. (2009). *Drive: The Surprising Truth About What Motivates Us.* New York: Penguin

Seligman, M. and Csikszentmihalyi, M. (2000) Positive psychology: An introduction.

American Psychologist, Vol 55(1), 5-14.

Smith, R. and Citrin, J. (2003). The 5 Patterns of Extraordinary Careers: The Guide for Achieving Success and Satisfaction. Publishers Weekly, Vol 250(27), 66.

Vroom, V. (1964). *Work and Motivation.* New York: Wiley.

INDEX

A

AGCT 88
Agreeableness is not "yes" men 78, 80
Aligning careers with your values 83
Aptitude and Skills Tools 87
Aptitude test
  Do not use if ... 93
Armed Services Vocational Aptitude Battery 87
Army Alpha test 87
Army General Classification Test 88
ASVAB 87, 88, 89

B

Baggage system in an airport 32
Be proactive rather than reactive 45
Best CV but not necessarily the best candidate 121
Big Hairy Audacious Goal (BHAG) 21, 29, 30, 63
Big Job Portal 76
Bolles, Richard 66, 135

C

Candle-stick maker story 46
Career elevator 57
Career search communication is about 120
Career Search System i, iii, 7, 41, 47, 66, 85, 95, 96, 103, 105, 110, 112, 191, 202, 203
  Focus Union 48, 50

Research stage 47
Career Shift 56
Collins, Jim 40
Conscientiousness 77, 78, 80
Culture and Companies 61

D

Differentiate YOUR information 134
DiSC 77, 78
Dominance, Influence, Steadiness, Conscientiousness 77

E

Excellent candidate for exploratory jobs 79
Expectancy theory 53
Extraversion 79

F

Find a Mentor 193
FIRE 4, 5, 6, 10, 37, 39, 43, 105
  Execute 6, 37
  Execution 43, 101
  Focus 5, 6, 37, 43, 44, 50, 99, 100
  Intensity 5, 6, 37, 43, 44, 99, 100
  Relationships 5, 6, 37, 43
First 90 days viii, 9, 16, 178, 193, 200, 201, 202, 205
  Short list of questions 201
Five Factor Model of Personality 78
Fuel system in your car 34

G

Glass ceiling 59
Good to Great 40, 233
Growth of Social Medium 133

H

Headhunters (aka Job Recruiters) 125
Hedgehog Principle 40, 41, 42
High level of attention to detail. 80

I

Informational interviews 63, 64
Internal exploration 19
Interviewing 159
   Categories of employment interview questions 161
   Challenge Action, Results 155
   crucial piece in the hiring process 98
   EXECUTION 101
   FOCUS 99
   How do I make it positive? 154
   INTENSITY 100
   RELATIONSHIP 101
   Using Soft Control 102, 155, 157, 159, 168

J

"Job-Task" Analysis 108

K

Kiersey-Bates Temperament Sorter 82
Kipling's "six honest serving men" 14
Know Thyself 66

L

Limited opportunities 18

M

Managing liabilities during the Interview 170

Redirection strategy 171
The "Iceberg" Technique 170
MBTI 81, 82
Meetings with recruiters 126
Mentor-protégé experience 194
Military careers 15
Myers Briggs Type Indicator 81

N

Navy General Classification Test 88
Negativity, Extraversion, Openness
  Personality Inventory 78
Negotiation is the act of communication 176
NEO-PI 78, 81
Networking viii, 141, 142, 145, 146, 151
  How do I make it work? 143
Networking cannot be overstated 148
Neuroticism 78
Non-profit sector 39, 67

O

Occupational Themes theory 73
O*Net 89
Openness 79
Organizational values 38

P

primary and secondary skills 18

R

Real deal on work/family balance 57
Recruiter placement statistics and success rates 126
Re-entering the Work Force 60

Résumé 96
  CARs 106, 111, 112, 118, 124, 168, 170, 172
  Executive Biography 98
  Expanded 97
  function 96
  Job Fair 97
  Job Fair Résumé 97, 148
  one-page is outdated 97
  purpose is to provide a quick idea 109
  value to white space 111
RIASEC 73, 76, 77
Right career vs. Best career 50, 51

S

Salary comparisons 180
Salary negotiation process 183
  basic framework 180
  benefit packages 184
  Bonuses 186
  cell phones, laptops, company cars 185
  First person to mention a Number loses 177
  Flexible Work Place 184
  Flexible Work Time 184
  Stock Options 186
Seligman, Martin 6
Send your recruiter career updates 128
Service Corps of Retired Executives (SCORE) 68
Set up a job agent 137
Small Business Administration (SBA) 68
Social Networking 146
Society for Human Resource Management 64
Soft control nets you the best package 103
Starting Your own Business 67

SYMLOG 84, 86
System for Multi-Level Observation of Groups 84

T

Technology enhanced networking tools 143
two-way loyalty 16
Types of Interviews
  Coworker Interview 164
  Initial Phone Call Interview 162
  One-on-one Interview 162
  Panel Interview 163
Types of Questions
  Behavioral Interview Questions 167
  Semi-Structured Interview Questions 166
  Situational Interview Questions 169
  Structured Questions 164

V

Values-Based Instruments 83
Vroom, Victor 53

W

What Color is Your Parachute? 66
What IS a career? 13
Why they need to hire someone 175
Will your personality fit within the team dynamic 164

www.ingramcontent.com/pod-product-compliance
Lightning Source LLC
LaVergne TN
LVHW051826080426
835512LV00018B/2747